Seth,

Dood +

I wish you the best of luck
and a productive life!

Q.C. #33

40 Days of Direction:
Life Lessons from the Talented Ten

DERRICK L. GRAGG, ED.D.

talentedten33@gmail.com

615-975-9873

DEDICATION

This book is dedicated to the two people most responsible for me being who I am - my parents. Whatever success I have had or will have in life, I owe to you. I thank you for never being my friends; you were always my PARENTS. You two taught me how to be a parent to my own children.

To "Ma," the woman who hasn't missed even one moment in my life since you brought me into this big world. Even when I was a little boy you always told me how "important" and successful I would become. You never set limits on what we could become, thus, we never set limits on ourselves. I love you.

To my Father, the man who was brave enough to go against Ma and get me involved in football again after my injury many years ago. I cannot imagine how life would be without you recognizing my passion for the game I have loved since I was three years old. And even though you are no longer here with us, I feel your presence on those fall Saturdays when I'm supporting my own team in a stadium somewhere in our great country. Continue to rest in peace...

FORWARD

With so much negativity surrounding student-athletes and young black males, this book is timely and necessary. We often hear about the athletes who run afoul of the law and squander golden opportunities. But, we rarely hear of the success stories. Forty Days of Direction from the Talented Ten is an insightful, engaging, and inspirational book about success.

Dr. Derrick Gragg's storytelling ability is superb. His capacity to integrate real stories and the important lessons learned from these stories is refreshing. Tens of thousands of student-athletes come to campuses throughout the nation poised with phenomenal athletic ability. However, few are equipped to deal with the overwhelming challenges of being both a student and an athlete. This book should be viewed as a manual for student-athletes. It candidly examines how to navigate the minefields of being a student-athlete. This book should be required reading for student-athletes across the nation.

On a personal level, I was a junior at Vanderbilt when Dr. Gragg and his classmates who dubbed themselves "DaFellaz" entered as freshman. I had the wonderful opportunity to see the evolution of their bond firsthand. As the leader of our football team, I mentored them as athletes. Off the field, I tried to set an example for them as students. I also pledged six of DaFellaz into Kappa Alpha Psi fraternity.

I was inspired by their positive energy and their will to help each other excel on and off the field. At that time, I had never witnessed such brotherhood. Their personalities were as separate as the five fingers but their spirits were one as the hand. I was there to witness two years' worth of the stories mentioned in this book. Dr. Gragg's accounts are riveting and accurate. Indeed, he is central to this incredible story. He was always the glue that held this group together.

The level of success that each one of them has achieved is stunning. And, as a group, their success is as remarkable as any group of friends that you could find. While we are quick to highlight failure in our society, this book is a celebration of achievement. Each one of the young men in this book is an iconoclast, an image-breaker. They have transcended stereotypes and found ways to achieve success against incredible odds.

In a time when academic and athletic administrators, educators, and coaches are grasping for solutions to a myriad of problems facing student-athletes, this book offers a substantive and empowering outline to overcome these challenges.

Renford Reese, Ph.D., Professor, Author
Founder, Colorful Flags

CONTENTS

ACKNOWLEDGMENTS

I cannot thank anyone until I thank my Lord and Savior. Although it is not politically correct to acknowledge God, I will always give You all the praise, honor and the glory You deserve. I am so humbled in Your presence and thank You for every chapter of my life, the good, the bad and the great ones. You blessed me with gifts I have been able to share with others. I pray that You will continue to bless me, my family and everyone who believes in You.

As always, an extra special thanks to my soul mate, best friend, confidant and biggest supporter, Sanya Whittaker Gragg. You have spent nearly two decades following me to some of the most "exotic" places in the world, including Fayetteville, Arkansas and Ypsilanti, Michigan. Thank you so much for giving up some of who you are so I could become who I am. Babe, you are my everything.

Thanks so much to DaFellaz, my inspirations for this book: Alex, Anthony, Carlos, Clarence, Corey, Derrick, Jason, Marcus, Oscar and William. You are the most talented, gifted, high-achieving group of men I have ever seen. I thank God for each of you and for putting us together in 1988. United we stand, divided we fall, forever and always my Brothers.

Special thanks to the father figures, my grandfathers. Granddad Gragg, my most important role model during my adult life. Thank you for showing me what a real man is. Granddad Smith, you were the backbone of our family for many years. Although you have been gone for a while, please know that I would never have become who I am without your support.

Thanks to my brothers T. Gragg and Phil. We played some of our best football against each other in the living room growing up. Love you Men.

Thanks to Dr. Renford Reese ("Dean Invincible"). You have always been my mentor, role model and the big brother I never had.

Thanks to John Lew, the best photographer in the state of Oklahoma. Your cover photo has given this project even more energy and life. Thank you to my editor, Lee Colony. I have always remembered the saying, "A book is only as good as its editor makes it," so I appreciate the work you put into this project. Special thanks to graphic designer Roderick Thompson for amazing cover design for this project. Special photo credit for the cover also goes to Embrick Johnson. Thanks men, I appreciate you.

I definitely want to acknowledge our Alma Mater Vanderbilt University and the Vanderbilt Department of Athletics. A special thank you to Ryan Schultz, Assistant Athletic Director/Communications for providing access to all the "old school" football action shots of us.

Finally to the young men coming up today who inspired me to write this book; I wrote this for YOU. Please read it closely and follow the advice within these pages. I am proud of you. I will meet you at the TOP!

TALENTED TEN MEMBERS OF "DAFELLAZ" ARE:

- Jason Brown, MBA – Executive Director, Head of Global Communications Compliance, J.P. Morgan Assets Management

- William Brown, Esq. – Lieutenant Colonel/Judge Advocate General (JAG)/U.S. Army

- Anthony Carter – Regional Technical Instructor, Comcast – Big South Region

- Dr. Derrick Gragg, Ed. D. – Vice President & Director of Intercollegiate Athletics, The University of Tulsa

- Corey Harris – Entrepreneur; Former NFL player, 12-year veteran, member of the Super Bowl Champion Baltimore Ravens

- Oscar L. Malone, Esq. – Attorney/Owner, Law Office of Oscar L. Malone III, P.C.

- Dr. Derrick Payne, DDS – Dentist, Owner, Superior Smiles, Memphis, TN

- Clarence Sevillian, MBA, MPT, FABC – CEO, McLaren Bay Region Hospital, Bay City, MI

- Dr. Carlos Thomas, Ph.D. – Director of Student Innovation Collaboratory (SICL) and former Chief Information Officer, Southern University, Baton Rouge, LA

- Alex Turner – Entrepreneur; Founder & Owner of The Homeboy Shoppin' Network (passed away on November 7, 1993)

- Marcus Wilson – Singer/Songwriter, toured with two Grammy-winning artists; currently pursuing Doctorate in physical therapy

INTRODUCTION

"It's not all about football. It's about the journey – mine and yours - and the lives we can touch, the legacy we can leave, and the world we can change for the better." – Tony Dungy

"Show me your friends and I'll show you your future." – Maurice Clarett, Former Ohio State Running Back and Motivational Speaker

TWENTY-SEVEN YEARS … That is how long I have been a part of "DaFellaz," a successful group of former teammates who have been lifelong friends, role models and BROTHERS. You never forget the day you meet someone who changes your life forever. For me, however, it wasn't just one person I met on that muggy, hot day in Nashville, Tennessee as I moved into the freshman dorm with the other ball players; it was 10 of them, all young men like me, ready to set the world on fire on the football field and educate ourselves at one of the top universities in the world.

Our story began in August of 1988 when I, along with 24 other starry-eyed freshmen, were introduced to the Vanderbilt University varsity football players as the "Class of 1992." We were all nervous and excited about going to college and playing football in the Southeastern Conference, arguably, the best football conference in the United States then and now. We were told to introduce ourselves to the entire team and then get acquainted with our freshmen classmates. I remember hearing the names of the young men who would become my lifelong friends - Corey Harris (my roommate), Derrick Payne, Carlos Thomas, Jason Brown, Marcus Wilson, Clarence Sevillian, Anthony Carter, William Brown and Oscar Malone. A few weeks later when the other students arrived on campus for the fall semester, we also met Alex Turner, Derrick Payne's best friend/high school classmate from Memphis, the only one of us who did not play football. At the time, I did not realize I had been introducing myself to such an important group of people, especially considering that many of us grew up poor – or in "broken" – homes without our biological fathers. At the time, our football class contained the largest number of African-Americans ever. There were 12 of us, so nearly half of our class was African-American. The three classes before us didn't have that many African-Americans COMBINED. From that moment on, 10 of us grew closer to one another as each day passed (one of the other African-Americans left within weeks of coming to Vandy and the other did not return after our freshman year).

There we stood, all of us black, most of us poor and from broken homes, enrolled at a private, predominantly white, Southern, upper-class university. We are all very proud of the fact that our football class has been ranked as one of the best in Vanderbilt history – but we also paid a heavy price personally and otherwise. Therefore, we did what was natural for this type of situation – we bonded. As the days, months and years passed, my teammates and I became more than friends, we became more like family, like brothers. We began calling ourselves "DaFellaz" of all things, loosely patterning ourselves after the group of rebellious young black men in Spike Lee's film "School Dayz." We were different from the other students at Vanderbilt and we knew it. We also embraced it.

Meeting, bonding and living with these guys for four years was the best educational experience of my life. Entering Vanderbilt, we were no different than many other ball players who go to college seeking NFL fame and fortune. However, as a group, we also understood the importance of education. Corey did achieve NFL success, playing 12 years in the league and becoming a Super Bowl champion. But, much more significantly, every one of the 10 of us graduated from college. Most of us also earned graduate degrees and have worked our way to the top of our individual professions, but none of us could have accomplished this without EACH OTHER and the many people whose shoulders we stand on today.

Although we are successful as a group, we have never forgotten where we came from and where we have been. Naturally, we are concerned about the young men of this generation and of the generations to come. We are very concerned with young black males, and the ball players today who continue to make national headlines -- and not in a GOOD way. Their actions, and repercussions, are life-altering. Simply put, young black men are in trouble. BIG trouble... High unemployment rates among young African-Americans, gang violence, the deterioration of public school systems across the country and even some hip hop/rap music are a few of the main culprits that have led to the demise of the African-American community. Due to poverty, racism, classism, and self-inflicted problems such as dropping out of school, having babies early in life despite having no education or income to care for the children, many young black males have no shot at living the "American dream." As the late rapper Notorious B.I.G. once said in his song *"Things Done Changed"*: "Either you're slinging crack rock or you got a wicked jump shot," meaning that young black kids from the 'hood only had two options for success, either by selling drugs or playing ball.

The enormous amounts of wealth professional athletes can obtain in this country causes athletics to often be seen as a possibility of escaping poverty and gaining a perceived acceptance in society for many African-Americans. However, the power of sport combined with EDUCATION should not be ignored. It is no secret that there are more young black men

11

in prisons than in college and rarely do we see African-American males shown as upstanding professional men, dedicated fathers and husbands. However, as many people know, black men like this DO exist – doctors, businessmen, lawyers, entrepreneurs and, yes, ball players. My closest friends and I are shining examples of what sports combined with education can do for a person. DaFellaz is a living example of this, as you will see in the pages to come.

Recently, while speaking at the third annual Emerging Administrators conference in Atlanta, I was asked what I believe is the biggest challenge facing college athletics. Is it paying the athletes? The arms race for bigger and better facilities? The high cost of coaching salaries and other expenses? None of these were my answer. Instead, I told them that the problem of student-athlete behavioral issues off the fields and courts of play is the most significant issue we face in college athletics today.

As a 22-year college athletics administrator at six major Division 1-A universities, I have talked to student-athletes about the many things that have the potential to cause them failure in college and in life. Unfortunately, I have been around student-athletes who have become distracted, flunked out of school and altered their lives forever. I have also read about many more student-athletes who have also self-destructed, many of whom are African-American.

So, I asked myself, "What can I do to help train, educate and motivate these young men and help them avoid the troubles that others before them did not avoid?" This book is at least a partial answer to this question. Even though I knew I could not always travel to spread positive messages and provide advice to the thousands of young people in from junior high through college, I still want to do SOMETHING. I also want my message to reach the family members, coaches and teachers who influence the student-athletes in their lives. The result? The book you are reading right now.

The stories and lessons in this book only provide an opportunity or a SHOT at success; no true blueprint leads to automatic success just by following the instructions. Nothing is guaranteed in this lifetime, but the messages contained in this book can certainly help young people dodge some of the pitfalls which have led others down the wrong path.

A few important things to keep in mind as you read this book and soak up its message:

- Each chapter ends with the opportunity for the reader to reflect on his own life and follow up on the issued challenge.

- The target audience is young males from junior high school through college along with their parents, grandparents, coaches, teachers and anyone else who is influential in their lives.

- While the key audience is African-American athletes, the book's message holds great meaning to young men of all races, to all athletes and to anyone seeking a better life and future.

- The book is also an important tool for everyone who loves, deals with, directs, coaches and instructs young men.

Over the years, "DaFellaz" have often reminisced about our days as often-defeated "gladiators" surviving on the football field and as African-American males, on an affluent and nearly all-white campus. We've also reminisced on our roles as fathers and husbands in today's society and our futures, collectively and individually. As a group, we feel like ground-breaking pioneers who burst open the doors for more African-Americans to be recruited, attend and play ball at one of the most prestigious universities in the world. As we reflect on days gone by and at how the past has undoubtedly shaped our lives, we realize the lessons we learned are invaluable, so invaluable, in fact, that we want to share them with everyone – especially the young men of the today's new generation. We don't expect you to sit down and read this entire book at one time. We want you to read a few pages a day/week, think about what you read and then put what you read into ACTION!

CHAPTER 1

YOU BELONG!

"Belief in oneself and knowing who you are, I mean, that's the foundation for everything great." Jay-Z

Don't be surprised if you feel you are different from many of the other students on campus, this is common. The fact is, you probably ARE different from most of your peers in many different ways. Since only a handful of high school athletes will be good enough athletically to earn a college athletic scholarship, you are already in elite company. If you are also an African-American male, you are certainly different than many of your peers. It is no secret that there are more black men in prison than in college - a VERY disturbing statistic. And even though you are in college (or on your way to college), as a young black man, you are also very different than most of the students on your campus because only about 3 percent of all college students are black men. Feeling different from the other students is one thing. Feeling that you don't belong is another matter altogether, though. Even if you feel you are "different," you should never feel that you do not belong, because you do. You BELONG.

I, along with other members of DaFellaz (my former college football teammates and best friends for life), attended Vanderbilt University, an elite, private, highly selective university in the deep South city of Nashville, Tenn. None of us would have been able to afford Vanderbilt had we not been on football scholarship. The cost of tuition, room and board, books and fees was more than $20,000 back then, (and has risen to more than $50,000 today). As a result, many of the students on campus came from families who were either upper middle class or just plain rich. For example, some of multimillionaire Ross Perot's children attended Vanderbilt, and at least one was there at the same time we were. If you don't know Ross Perot, he is a businessman worth about $3.7 billion – yes BILLION – who ran for president of the United States twice during the 1990's. Yet, despite the fact that we did not have the cars, clothes, and other things many of our peers had, we still felt that we belonged. And no one could tell us otherwise.

So, you didn't score a perfect 1600 on your SAT exam to get into college. And yes, the fact that you run faster and jump higher than most people on campus helped you get where you are today. But please, NEVER let anyone tell you that you do not BELONG where you are right now. According to statistics, there are more than 1.2 million high school football players. But only about 3,000 of these players sign a national letter of intent to play for a Division I (FBS) University and another 2,300 at the Division I-AA (FCS) level. This means that less than 1% of the players will earn a football scholarship to attend college. You have already overcome major hurdles to get where you are. YOU BELONG!

There will be students and professors on campus who believe you go to college for free, don't have to go to class or don't do anything you don't want to do. Some will feel that all you have to do is get ready for the game and then find ways to kill time until next week's game. Make sure you compete in the classroom with as much passion as you compete on the field or court. You are an athlete, which means you are naturally competitive and want to win. So, win in the classroom! Never forget that YOU BELONG! I have learned that employers often value your experiences as a student-athlete. They know you had to handle your classes and professors, the demands of your coaches and the physical and mental stress created by college sports. Right now, you may have very few (or none) of the material things other students have. You may not drive a nice vehicle, live in a "plush" apartment or have a big bank account. But if you stay the course, work hard and keep your FOCUS, one day you'll have all the things you need, want and more. There is a reason you are one of the very few people who are where you are today. You BELONG!

CHALLENGE: Today I challenge you to look at yourself in the mirror and say, "I belong here and no one is going to stop me from graduating and becoming successful in life! I and others have worked hard to get me here. I belong and I will not fail!"

Dr. Carlos Thomas, Marcus Wilson, Clarence Sevillian & Dr. Derrick Payne, 1992 – Photo Credit: Vanderbilt Athletics

CHAPTER 2

NFL - NOT FOR LONG/NBA: NO BOYS ALLOWED

"I always tell people, I can stuff a ball through a hoop, but I also have a mind." - Kareem Abdul-Jabbar

Corey Harris, 12 Year NFL Veteran, 1992-2003
Photo Credit: NFL.com

I will never forget the first time I saw my former college teammate and roommate, Corey Harris, on the football field. Our incoming freshman football class was practicing without the varsity players (back in the "old days" of 1988, the freshmen players weren't allowed to practice with the older players until they practiced with other freshmen for three or more days) and I began watching Corey closely. I had heard that he was good, but I didn't know he was THAT good. Before our first practice, I felt a little superior to the rest of my freshman teammates because I had been on campus for six weeks participating in a summer pre-engineering program and working out with the older varsity players. I felt that I had the upper hand, since I was the only one of the 20-plus new players who already "knew the ropes." I had a little "swagger" when my classmates showed up for the first days of official college workouts. However, it didn't take long for me to realize that there were some other very talented young "hot shots" in our class, especially my roommate, Corey Harris.

In our four years at Vandy, Corey did everything except, as they say, sell popcorn at games. He played receiver, ran back kickoffs, ran back punts and played running back. After three years of being used as a "utility guy" who was plugged in to do whatever we needed him to do, our new head coach, Gerry DiNardo, did something that no coach before him had done: He allowed Corey to play running back. And MAN, could he play running back. None of us were surprised at his 12-year NFL career. If there was ever an athletic "freak of nature," Corey was certainly one. And so was nearly everyone else who played with and against him in the NFL. That is why I sometimes laugh to myself when every hand goes up in the room of college football players when they are asked the question, "Who wants to play in the NFL?"

Just like everyone else I played ball with, I, too, wanted to be a great NFL player, the next John Stallworth or Lynn Swann. And, while I was one of the best football players in my high school's history, I turned out to be just an average college player, and nearly all my teammates AND our opponents were, too. The VERY few exceptions who were blessed with much more athletic ability got a CHANCE to play pro ball. Notice that I said a CHANCE, because there were certainly no guarantees then, none now, and there will never be any guarantee.

Are you being REALISTIC about playing in the NFL after college? I'm not telling you to give up on your dreams. I would never do that. I do encourage you to pursue other interests outside sports and take full advantage of your opportunities to network in college.

When growing up, many young boys/men dream of one day taking care of their parents – their mothers, in particular – and making life easier for them. However, the allure of professional football is perhaps the greatest deterrent to academic success for many student-athletes. Out of the approximately one million high school football players in the United States annually, the most who will ever sign a professional football contract and play ball in the NFL each year is about 150. Many times it's fewer. Even those who make it to the "big dance" will only play an average of 3 to 4 years (which is why we all hear about the saying: NFL - NOT FOR LONG). Chances of making the NBA are even slimmer.

I truly hope that all student-athletes will begin to understand the importance of getting a degree while in college. Playing college ball is a great honor and a privilege and is certainly one of the main reasons I am where I am today. However, my education is an even bigger reason why I am here today. As I mentioned, my man Corey played in the NFL for 12 years. Corey compares playing in the NFL to winning the lottery. He often says that even though one person will "win" (make it to the NFL), the other 99 percent attempting to do the same thing will never realize their dreams of making it to the league. Although there will always be a few winners, the majority will lose. The question is: How long are you willing to play, hoping to win that lottery?

CHALLENGE: Today I challenge you to be realistic about your true chances of playing in the NFL/NBA and make more of a commitment to educating yourself. I'm not saying forget about pro ball totally, but don't let it control you. Sports will only last for moment, but the education and skills you gain from a college degree will last a lifetime.

CHAPTER 3

SHAKE THE HATERS AND CHASE YOUR DREAMS: GO HARD OR GO HOME!

"A great pleasure in life is doing what people say you cannot do." – Walter Bagehot

Have you ever noticed how negative some people can be? I'm sure most of you have at least one "friend" or family member who is constantly whining and complaining about anything and everything. But, you should never listen to anyone who tells you what you CANNOT do. These people are critics who may not have your best interests in mind. In other words, they are not really your friends and do not wish for good things to happen to or for you. You will notice that most of the time, critics are people who haven't done much to distinguish themselves in life. The word used most often to describe today's critic is the word HATER. They are also usually jealous and envious of people they secretly admire and never do big things themselves; instead, they sit around and talk negatively about people who are actually DOING things. Not only should you dream big, you must do everything you can to work on your dreams to make them come true. So what if you are "too young," "too inexperienced," "not connected to the right people," "unpopular," etc.? If you want it, GO AND GET IT!

Perhaps the most significant example in our lifetime of someone dreaming big and succeeding against all odds is President Barack Obama. I must admit I never thought I would live to see the day a black man would become the president of the United States and the most powerful person in the free world. President Obama refused to allow our country's history slow him down or make him turn away from his dream. I can only imagine the negative things he heard when he began sharing his dreams with other people, even those close to him. But look at him NOW! The great thing is that President Obama is no different than me and you. He is no different because at one time, like you, he was a young person trying to find his way.

I am also a great example of someone who has overcome odds to reach my dreams at an early age. Like you, I have encountered a number of haters throughout my entire lifetime. When I went to Vanderbilt on an athletic scholarship, I heard that I was only allowed to attend school there because I was on the football team. When I got into law school, I heard that I was only admitted because the school needed more black students. When I got my first job in college athletics at the age of 23, I heard that I was "too young" for the job and I really only got the job because my old football coach wanted me to have it. When I became the youngest athletic director in the country, I heard that I was selected for the position because

the school wanted to hire a minority. The list goes on and on.

I have learned over the years that the best way to deal with haters is to keep doing the things that made them hate you in the first place! Keep being who you are and doing what got you this far in life. The haters were not up with you at 5 a.m. running sprints and lifting weights. The haters were not there with you when you stayed up all night studying for an important exam. The haters will not cheer you on when you walk across that stage on graduation day to accept your diploma from the school president, when you work 12-hour days to support your family, or even when you become a partner in a law firm. Some people are ALWAYS waiting to dislike you or label you as "unworthy." Dream big anyway!

Always remember these simple rules regarding those who attempt to limit you and cause you to stray from your dreams:

- Don't focus on people who criticize you. Instead, focus on those who are positive and supportive. Being successful is what's most important.

- Pursuing dreams you may never reach is MUCH better than having no dreams at all.

- Marten Patrick Fitch, one of my best friends and fraternity brothers, once said to me, "God won't give you a basketball jersey, shorts and a ball, and not put you in the game! If He has given us the tools to prepare us, then surely He has His loving eyes on us and knows when we are ready for the starting lineup." I agree 100%.

- When you do "big" things, you will find that not everyone will celebrate you or your success, regardless of the positive impact you make. Simply put, like President Obama, your dreams may be too big for everyone to understand or support. Dream big ANYWAY!

If everyone took the haters in their lives seriously, none of us would ever reach the heights that are in store for us. Continue to dream big and chase your dreams. And even if you do fail, at least fail giving it all you have every single day, instead of sitting on the sidelines with the haters.

CHALLENGE: Today I challenge you to ignore the haters who don't want you to succeed. Putting your thoughts and energy into people who aren't on your "team" will only drain you. Focus on where you want to go, not on the people or obstacles in that stand in your way. Ignore anyone who attempts to limit your vision and keep you in a "box"! You can accomplish ANYTHING!

CHAPTER 4

#24 DR. DERRICK PAYNE, WINGBACK -
"THE ROLE MODEL"

"Success is to be measured not so much by the position that one has reached in life as by the obstacles which he has overcome." — Booker T. Washington

It's an old saying, but all of us who have played football or any other high speed or contact sport have heard it before: "It only takes one play to end your career." This was definitely the case for DaFellaz member, Derrick Payne. "D. Payne," as we still call him, was blessed with cat-like quickness and a burst of speed unlike any I'd seen. This guy was so good he seemed to return at least 1 out of every 2 punts for touchdowns in practice and we all felt he was destined for the NFL. However, that all ended on a muggy Saturday night down in Starkville, Miss., when D. Payne tore a major ligament in his knee. There to witness the tragedy were his mother and many other family members who traveled from Memphis to see his debut as our starting tailback and punt returner against Mississippi

State. His entire season ended in that game. He gained 54 yards on 12 carries… Game over right? WRONG!!!

When D. Payne went down in that game, his educational and professional career goals did not go down with him. Since the day I met him, he worked extra hard when it came to school and books. In fact, I would rank D. Payne as one of the more serious students within our clique during college. Now, don't get me wrong — he LOVED to party and "hang" just like the rest of us, but there was still something a bit different about him. Like many young black men, D. Payne was raised by a single mother and his grandmother. After he was injured at Mississippi State on that Saturday night, D. Payne's mother packed up her things early that Sunday morning and moved to Nashville. Little did anyone know, she actually had no place to stay but lived in the study room of our dorm a few weeks before she found a small apartment near campus. Since we were all on full scholarship, we'd often get extra food to take back to the dorm for her. As the old saying goes, "there's no love like a mother's love"!!!!

After months of hard work to rehab his knee, and despite being a step slower, D. Payne was ready to play the following year. He worked even harder on the field, but he was obviously not the same athlete he was prior to his injury. In the classroom, he studied hard, and after graduation, went on to the University of Tennessee at Memphis Dental School. Similar to the road he traveled as an undergraduate, he also encountered very challenging times as a dental student. He told me that he felt like giving up at times, but his drive and will to succeed would not let him quit. Today it is no surprise that Dr. Derrick Payne is now a prominent dentist in his hometown. He now owns two dental offices in Memphis and was named

"Best Dentist" in the city in both 2013 and 2015 at the "Best in Black" awards event which is sponsored by The New Tri-State Defender newspaper. His mother has even worked with him in past years as his personal assistant. Now how is THAT for a poor boy from Memphis, Tennessee? D. Payne is a true hometown hero, a success story and a true role model for young men all over the country and the world who are attempting to beat the odds and overcome major obstacles to succeed in life.

Some athletes will "retire" right after their last high school or college game. Others may be fortunate enough to make it to the league for a few years. Remember, though, that 3 years is the average NFL life for ball players and 5 years is the average for those in the NBA. You, too, must retire when the ball "goes flat." What are YOU going to do when you "retire?" Like D. Payne, you should ALWAYS have a backup plan! No matter what stage you are at in your life right now, you are probably engaging in something that you will retire from eventually. So use this chapter as a guide to make sure you are preparing yourself for the inevitable.

CHALLENGE: People's journeys to success are never easy, but always remember the difficult times you face and use them as motivation to stay on the path to success. Today I challenge you to work harder on your goals and plans for life after your playing days are over.

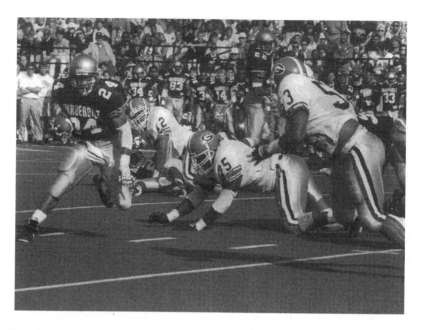

Dr. Derrick Payne after his knee injury, carrying ball in Vanderbilt's 1991 27-25 win over Georgia - Photo Credit: Vanderbilt University Athletics

CHAPTER 5

COLLEGE IS NO PLACE FOR A GANGSTER

"In their songs and in their gangster personae, some rappers promote the notion that you're lame if you go to school; you're weak if you weren't raised slinging dope; you're nobody if you didn't come up hard." – Nathan McCall

In today's society, the art of "keeping it real" has gone to new levels where it seems that everybody wants to be a gangster, including hip hop stars and ball players. As someone who was a teenager during what is referred to as the "Golden Age of Hip Hop," I was in high school when rap music exploded onto the mainstream through Grandmaster Flash & the Furious Five, Run DMC, KRS-1 and LL Cool J. By the time I was in college more radical rappers like Public Enemy, KRS-1 and N.W.A. dubbed "the world's most dangerous group" had taken over the airwaves. And throughout the years since then, I have seen ground-breaking artists like Tupac Shakur, the Notorious B.I.G. Jay-Z, Eminem, Lil Wayne, Drake and Kendrick Lamar make it big in the music world. Throughout its growth, hip hop music has been closely tied to big-time athletics. The large amount of hip hop music played at football stadiums and basketball arenas across the country is a great example of hip hop's influence on sport. Many teams even practice with hip hop music playing over the sound system. Today, not only is Jay-Z arguably the greatest rapper alive, he also founded Roc Nation Sports, a sports agent company that represents big-time athletes such as Kevin Durant, Dez Bryant and Victor Cruz.

Perhaps the first memorable collaboration of hip hop and sport was the University of Michigan players known as "The Fab Five," who became cultural icons and trendsetters with their bald heads, long, baggy shorts, black socks and confident swagger on the court. They also all loved the hip hop of the early 1990's. These guys were revolutionaries who received racist hate mail from Michigan fans and alumni who did not agree with the way they played the game of basketball and carried themselves on and off the court. And they all loved hip hop music and helped push it further into mainstream American culture. NBA ballers Allen Iverson, Shaquille O'Neal, Chris Webber and Kobe Bryant took it even further and recorded hip hop records.

In the late 1980's, the hip hop movement started to become more violent in tone. What started out as a competitive, free and fun form of lifestyle has drifted into a world of "gangsterism," of violence, drugs, money, sex and murder. While Public Enemy, N.W.A. and Tupac Shakur directed their anger and rage toward injustice, police brutality and "the establishment," many men of color direct their anger and rage toward EACH OTHER. Athletes were not immune to this violence and have also been involved in the rage and violence as victims or voluntarily became wrongdoers who victimized others.

Unfortunately, ball players have been convicted of serious crimes including murder and are spending the rest of their lives in prison. On the college level student-athletes have died as victims of violence (Auburn, UConn and Eastern Michigan - where I was the athletic director for seven years). Yes, athletes - even well-known, wealthy athletes - go to jail and they have also been victims of violence. Some paid the biggest price of all – they lost their lives. When at school or on a college campus you have to remember that you may also be around people in the community who aren't students. You may find yourself in the middle of a dangerous situation like someone waving a gun around at a party threatening other people there. Remember, you are not bullet-proof.

1. Avoid high crime areas near your school and especially in your hometown when you visit.

2. Remember that the music you listen to is just that – MUSIC. Many of the rappers who talk about drug-dealing, making fast money and killing people have never done ANY of those things. In the end, you have to be able to recognize and separate fantasy from reality.

3. Always report dangerous things you hear or see to your coaches. The coaches WANT and NEED to hear this type of information. It is better to be a "snitch" than to bury one of your teammates.

4. Distance yourself from friends of others you grew up with if they are involved with situations and activities that can get you into big trouble. Real friends would never put you at risk or get you into situations that can ruin your career.

CHALLENGE: Today I challenge you to stay clear of the traps that so many other young people fell into. Protect yourself and protect the investment of your time, sweat and hard work that you have put in to get here. College is no place for a gangster.

CHAPTER 6

DON'T GET YOURSELF INTO TROUBLE
YOU CAN'T GET OUT OF

"It takes a great deal of bravery to stand up to your enemies, but a great deal more to stand up to your friends." Albus Dumbledore, *Harry Potter and the Sorcerer's Stone*

*Names in this chapter have been changed in this chapter to protect the VERY foolish...

"Run!!! Runnnn!!! "Steve" yelled to our teammates as he hobbled quickly down the stairs on crutches in the "Towers" dorm on campus. "5-0 is here man, RUN!!! Get out of there and let's G-O-O-O-O!!!" Soon after Steve's warning, campus police began swarming our dorm because of a break-in that occurred in the small grocery store (or Munchi Mart as it was called) on the lower level of the building. The Munchi Mart was the students' saving grace back then since we did not have access to the same types of on-campus restaurants that today's college students enjoy. Since "The Mart," as we called it, stayed open until midnight, we could head downstairs to find a late night snack, which happened a lot with us football players. However, this night was different. Someone had broken into our beloved Munchi Mart... Little did I know that the lawbreakers were some of my best friends and teammates...

"Hold on, tell me again... Yall fools did WHAT last night??!!" I asked Frank as we sped down the highway to perform in a big statewide Greek Show in Birmingham, Alabama I couldn't believe what I was hearing...

Frank said, "Man, I told you... Last night we broke into the Munchi Mart dude. And the police showed up! Man, I ran all the way up to the 14th floor to get away when I heard that the cops they were coming!

32

"I can't believe you agreed to go along with that man, I really can't. Frank, you're one of our best players! What were you THINKING?!"

"Obviously I was thinking about stocking up my fridge and closet with food for days Frat," Frank responded. "But I'm glad we listened to you when you told us before we did anything that stupid that we'd better have a plan."

That comment took me back to the night before when my boys were congregating in one of our fraternity brother's dorm rooms to plan what became known as the infamous "Munchi Mart Caper" to the members of our clique. One of my boys had actually found the key to the store because the employee who closed the store that night had mistakenly left the key in the lock. So instead of my teammate doing the right thing and turning in the key, he kept it. And the Munchi Mart Caper was born.

"Man, DG, you're always so scared and paranoid," one of my teammates yelled to me after I told them that robbing the place was the most ridiculous thing I'd ever heard of. "We're not going to get caught. Man, we have the KEY to the place. This will be easy!"

"Let me get this straight," I responded, "Yall are going down there to steal something that we can get for FREE every week? Call me what you want, but I'm not going to be in the middle of this, my dudes. You shouldn't do this. Whatever you do, you better get a plan together," I said as I exited the room, hopped on the elevator and went back to my own room.

I actually thought that they had listened to me and decided against taking a chance at becoming convicted felons. It turned out that they listened, but only to the part where I told them to make sure they had a plan — not the part where I told them it was stupid to even think of doing something that crazy. And don't get me wrong, I was definitely no "saint" in college. However, the one thing I knew I could not do was lose my football scholarship, especially over something as ridiculous as robbing a store where we got to "purchase" $90.00 worth of food and other stuff weekly by using our student IDs. Of all the "perks" that athletes enjoyed, this was certainly the best one in my book. And I wasn't about to screw it all up. Remember, someone has to be the voice of reason when your friends, teammates, fraternity brothers or family members are about to make mistakes that could change their lives forever.

Of course I didn't reveal the real names of the guys who were in on that foolishness; fortunately they all ended up being very successful, prominent individuals representing some of the most honorable professions in the country. But that night, they were guys who thought they could get away with something illegal, acting stupid. One of the guys jumped in the large ice chest in the storage room near the Munchi Mart in the basement of the dorm and began frantically covering himself with ice when the police showed up. ICE??!! Not very smart for a guy who was an honor student. Another one of my boys ended up lying to police who caught him in the laundry room near the Munchi Mart. At least he was smart enough to actually have some of his clothes washing and drying so that he had a semi-believable alibi. To this day, he is still thanking me for convincing them to have a plan. It was a true miracle that my friends did not get caught trying to steal things that we got each week for "free."

When several of DaFellaz got together, we talked about that crazy night. One of the guys said that they were just "having a little fun" that night and never thought it was a serious situation – until the police showed up of course. That night my friends put their futures, their family names, our football program and our fraternity in jeopardy. What my boys failed to grasp that night is that the world can be quite unforgiving to guys who make mistakes in life, especially to those who are viewed as "privileged athletes who wouldn't be on campus if they couldn't play ball"... Therefore, had they been caught, it is safe to say that some — if not all — of them would have been thrown off the team and out of school. Had that happened, where would they be NOW? Since they are all very intelligent men (minus the night they broke into the Munchi Mart), maybe they could have rebounded and turned out exactly how they are today... But I seriously doubt it.

CHALLENGE: Today I challenge you to eliminate making mistakes that could cost you your future, especially mistakes that could lead to jail or prison. Distance yourself from "friends" who always seem to find and create trouble before it's too late. We all make mistakes, but the key to life is not making the mistakes that can ruin your life. Real talk...

DERRICK L. GRAGG, ED.D.

CHAPTER 7

REMEMBER, SHE IS SOMEONE'S DAUGHTER

"A woman brought you into this world so you have no right to disrespect one." – Tupac Shakur

There are too few positive portrayals of women on television today, especially those who appear on reality shows. Characterizations of women of color on television are even worse, sometimes MUCH worse. I often feel sorry for those women, despite the fact that they are making a profit from selling out in front of thousands, even millions, of people who watch the shows each week. There is nothing worse than seeing a beautiful, intelligent woman disrespect herself and those around her. All you have to do is turn on a hip hop music video or one of the several awful reality television shows to see women degrading themselves shaking it for the cameras and the audiences. Music videos portray women as booty-shaking sex-kittens or materialistic gold-diggers. Many of those women simply do not seem to have sense of self and who they REALLY are or where they came from at all. However, regardless of what you see or hear, there are very good, upwardly mobile, smart women out there. You probably encounter them every day at school or in the community.

Even when you encounter a female who seems to disrespect herself, be respectful and treat her like a lady. In other words, no matter what, be a gentleman. Always remember that no matter how a woman may look on the outside, she is someone's daughter. Treat women the way you want your own mother to be treated by your father, stepfather or any man with whom she has a relationship. You all have sisters, aunts, daughters,

36

grandmothers, nieces and female cousins. As men, you should treat women the way you want your own female family members treated.

I know that it can be very difficult to be a gentleman at all times. We usually have only seconds to make some of the most important decisions that can ultimately change the way our lives turn out. I know it's tough. The alcohol is flowing, she is "feeling" you and you are definitely feeling her. This is why it is critical for you to THINK during these times. There have been many situations where athletes, fraternity members and other male students have found themselves caught up in very serious situations involving women, including sexual assault, violence and rape. Recently, several football and basketball student-athletes at big-time programs have been accused of violent crimes against women such as rape and assault. They have been thrown off their teams and out of college and ultimately may end up in prison for many years. Just imagine how much these athletes' lives have changed in a few months, from running out of the locker room to the sound of thousands of fans, to the unthinkable life that prison may bring. I'm sure they would give anything to go back to the situation with those women that led them down that road. I'm sure that they would do anything to change the circumstances and would not be anywhere close to the young ladies involved. But unfortunately, life doesn't happen like that.

Remember, she is someone's daughter. Treat her and all women with respect at ALL times. If you cannot do that, stay away from her and focus on the other things going on in your life. In the end, you could save your future and your life – and hers as well.

CHALLENGE: Today I challenge you to treat women with the same respect as your own mother, grandmother sisters, aunts, or daughter. Remember that every woman you encounter is someone's daughter who deserves to be treated with respect.

CHAPTER 8

#2 MARCUS WILSON, QUARTERBACK – "THE SHOW STOPPER"

"To be a star you must shine your own light, follow your own path and don't worry about the darkness. For that is when the stars shine brightest." – Unknown

Marcus "Doc" Wilson, "My Quarterback" as I will always refer to him, is without a doubt the most multi-talented man I know. Like several of the other Fellaz, he was a dynamic athlete who could make things happen when he had the football. Although he "rode the pine" behind other quarterbacks the first three years we were in college, when he was finally given the starting nod at QB, he went to WORK. During our fourth year, Doc led the Southeastern Conference (SEC) in scoring with 11 touchdowns. He also is still number two on the Vanderbilt all-time rushing touchdown list. Of course, we still tell him the only reason he scored so many times was that he was a ball hog who always carried the ball himself near the goal line instead of pitching it to Corey or Ace.

Doc finally got his just due, but the beginning of Doc's career at Vandy was a bumpy one. Believe it or not, having a black starting quarterback was unpopular and many times unaccepted – especially in the SEC. Eric Jones – Vandy's only Heisman Trophy candidate, who is also African-American – was the starting quarterback our freshman year. As I recall, though, Eric was the ONLY starting black quarterback in the conference at that time. Of course that has changed dramatically in recent years as quarterbacks like Cam Newton at Auburn, Blake Sims at Alabama and Dak Prescott at Mississippi State led their teams to great success.

Although Doc was a very talented football player, I was more impressed with his skills off the field. The first time I heard him singing in the freshman dorm, I was blown away – literally. And his dance moves were even BETTER. The guy could move like Chris Brown and sing like Anthony Hamilton. Doc was in a word – DIFFERENT. The same way Corey was different from us on the field, Doc was different from us OFF the field. His talent was just that overwhelming. So overwhelming that I and four more of DaFellaz quickly formed a singing group around him and began doing talent shows on campus.

Many of DaFellaz came from very humble beginnings, but in addition to growing up poor, Doc's father left the family when Doc was about 6 years old. According to Doc, his father "got up one day to go to the store and never came back."

"People say 'Wow, Marcus you grew up without a father," and I tell them, "Well no, he actually RAISED ME. The fact that he left, the mistakes that he made, the things that he DIDN'T teach me helped me to become a man," Doc said.

Maybe that's why Doc was so tough, so driven and so eager to show how good he was at everything. Like many talented black singers, he began singing in the church at a young age and never stopped. After we graduated from college and attempted a short-term run at being a legitimate group, Doc continued in the music industry as a singer and songwriter and became one of lead singers for the legendary gospel music icon Bobby Jones's Nashville Super Choir. He also toured with 5-time Grammy nominated R&B artist Regina Belle who won a Grammy for her duet "A Whole New World" with Peabo Bryson, which was the

blockbuster hit on the *Aladdin* movie soundtrack.

Just like way back in 1988 when we met, Doc has STAR POWER. He's the guy in the room you can tell is special. What I learned most from him was to never make excuses (see my other chapter Excuses, Excuses, Excuses) and to do what you have to do to get people's attention to display the talent you have. If you're a talented writer, then don't waste time trying to become an engineer. If you're a math whiz, don't become an English professor. Be who you ARE and not who someone else wants you to be. Doc was a QUARTERBACK, not a receiver, and although it took him three long years to convince the coaches, he earned that starting job and never let it go. He also never let that ball go when we were on the goal line! And although Doc never became the multi-platinum star since marriage, children and supporting his family led him down a different pathway, he can bring the house down with a song better than many of the famous musical stars I've seen over the years. I wouldn't be surprised if he someday releases a solo CD, either R&B, or gospel or both. In the meantime, Doc is pursuing his doctorate in physical therapy while continuing to bless those around him with his talent like he does on the Sundays he sings in church. What is your talent, your gift?

CHALLENGE: Remember that not all stars perform on stages. Today I challenge you to become a "star" at what you do best. Don't allow anyone to stop you from using your true talents to take you where you want to be.

Marcus Wilson (top right) as lead singer of college singing group with classmate James Sanders (front left) and teammates Dr. Derrick Payne (front right), Corey Harris (middle) and Dr. Derrick Gragg (top left)

Marcus Wilson singing to his bride Tina at their wedding

CHAPTER 9

WHAT ABOUT YOUR FRIENDS?

"You can often tell how far your life and career will go based on the five people you spend the most time with." – Will Smith

In 1992, during my senior year in college, the mega-female group TLC released their debut album, *Oooooooh...On the TLC Tip*. The all-girl group was considered groundbreaking because of their edginess and willingness to talk about issues in their songs that other female artists dared not touch back then. Their first song, *I Ain't 2 Proud 2 Beg*, was an immediate hit because it touched on the liberation of women who weren't afraid to ask men for what they wanted in bed. Like other young men at the time, I thought the song was bold and thought-provoking (and it didn't hurt that the three members of the group were all very attractive). However, my favorite song from the album was called *"What About Your Friends."* As a music lover who loves to dance, I first began liking the song because of its hard-thumping beat; however, the more I listened to it, the more I began to think about the message of the song. The chorus of the song reads:

What about your friends?

Will they stand their ground?

Will they let you down again?

What about your friends?

Are they gonna be low down?

Will they ever be around?

Or will they turn their backs on you?

The song is about being able to rely on people close to you. I am always thankful that I was able to find the best friends anyone could ever have while I was still very young. Even before college I was blessed with

44

three lifelong friends from my hometown who are still with me today: Richie Carter, Technical Director, Digital Maintenance Environment Aviation Programs at 4M Research, Inc.; Melvin Hines, long-time college sports administrator who serves as the athletic director at Alabama State University and Michael Massey, a career military man who retired from the Air Force after serving our country for many years. Then DaFellaz came into my life at 18 years of age and changed it forever. Even when we met back in 1988, it was very obvious to me that these guys were special. I am sure that as a group, Da Fellaz is one of the most successful groups of former college football players in the history of the game. Among us are a dentist who owns two dental offices; a Super Bowl champion; two attorneys – one who is a major/judge advocate general in the U.S. Army; a university instructor who holds not one, but two Ph.Ds.; one of the youngest CEOs of a hospital in the country; a vice president of a major bank on Wall Street in New York; a gifted singer/song-writer; and the youngest African-American Division IA athletic director in the country. That's not bad for a group of "washed up" athletes. Of course, this group of men is far from perfect (see the earlier chapter about the "Munchi Mart" robbery), but we were able to learn from our mistakes and help each other continue to push forward during critical times in our lives. THAT is what true friendship is all about.

If you are not surrounded by the right friends or people who are like you, who can help you get where you are trying to go, I encourage you to find other people. At least find just one other person who is more like you and who wants to succeed in life and make a difference. Start now, and do it TODAY. Remember, if you're always the smartest, most talented person in your inner circle, you need to change your circle.

CHALLENGE: Today I challenge you to begin — or continue — to surround myself with winners in all aspects of their lives. Surround yourself with people who are working hard ever to make something of themselves. Work to become a better friend yourself as well.

* Rest in Peace, Lisa "Left Eye" Lopes of the super-group TLC. (Song lyrics written by Dallas Austin and Lisa Lopes).

Dr. Gragg, Anthony Carter, Corey Harris, Clarence Sevillian

CHAPTER 10

PULL THOSE PANTS UP! YOUR APPEARANCE MATTERS!!!

"If you have embraced a thug image, how can you blame the system for treating you in the same way that you portray yourself? If you look like and behave like a thug, people will treat you as a thug." – Dr. Renford Reese

"Pull those pants up, boy!" I can still hear my Grandmother's voice echoing in my head. How many times have some of us heard that same phrase or similar phrases from our parents/grandparents or any other adult who felt we were getting out of line? Of course, today's generation is much different than ours was. Adults are not "allowed" to correct the young people today. However, you should know that even though no one may be correcting you, people are watching and judging you. Always remember that what you wear says a LOT about you. There is nothing like seeing a young man on campus or in the community that is neatly dressed and looks like a college student. There is also nothing like seeing a student on campus wearing a baseball cap backwards, pants sagging, and earphones, blasting music with music blaring loud enough for everyone to hear. The biggest question is: Who do you want to be?

Never lose your identity and a sense of who you really are or where you came from, but always remember WHERE YOU ARE. You are in a world of learning, education and culture, oftentimes, a culture far different from your own. However, you must learn to function properly in the new environment and do what you are in school to do. While you may be unable to afford designer clothing or the most expensive sneakers, you can still take pride in your appearance. You can always "dress up" your appearance by tucking in your shirt, making sure your shoes are clean and polished and never, ever allowing your pants to sag and hang down exposing your underwear. I would much rather see a person wearing a no-name brand of clothing and shoes that look respectable rather than seeing a guy's $300 jeans falling down around his ankles when he walks.

Remember that many times, due to your size and the color of your skin (if you attend a predominantly white institution), you and many other African-American student-athletes are already very noticeable on college campuses and unable to "blend in" to mainstream society like many of the people around you. I know this for a fact because I and my best friends and teammates dealt with the same thing when we were in college. Simply put, you cannot hide! So since you cannot hide, cover up and blend in on campus, you need to stand out in other ways – POSITIVE ways. You should also remember that many times you are not judged as an individual when you do not represent yourself properly; you are also causing people to judge your teammates and friends because young men of color are often judged COLLECTIVELY. In other words, some people in society view all young black men the same way, especially when the young men are "acting a fool," "wilding out" and doing things that can lead to a lot of trouble.

In my past experiences I have witnessed bias based on student-athlete appearance first-hand. Upon seeing an unshaven African-American male student-athlete in my office who wore today's popular "hip hop" attire and a wild, uncombed afro hairstyle, a colleague asked me, "Who was *that?* He looks like a thug! He should go home and comb his hair!" My colleague did not know that the young man was probably the most intelligent and articulate student-athlete on the entire football team. She did not know that this young man has the two most highly educated, fascinating parents of any color I have ever met during my 20-plus years as an athletic administrator. She also did not know that he had just met with me about setting up a meeting for all the African-American males on campus to discuss pressing issues. Therefore, I called the young man back into my office so that he could introduce himself to my colleague. After speaking to her for 15 minutes, she asked him to accompany her back to her office where they spent the next hour talking. When the young man left her office my colleague told me that she had never encountered a more articulate, well-spoken, dynamic student. I made this illustration to point out peoples' perceptions are their reality. Had I not introduced the student-athlete to my colleague, her initial perception of the young man – young black thug - would have been her reality.

Luckily for him, I was able to help him change the administrator's opinion by having them talk. However, this won't be the case in many similar situations. The first impression you make with a professor or anyone else on campus will often be the only impression that matters.

If you do not know what you should wear on campus, here is some strong advice from me, a person who has been on a college campus almost every day since 1988 as either a student or athletic administrator and an instructor teaching classes on several campuses:

1. There is nothing worse — in my opinion — than a young man wearing any type of hat or baseball cap once he has gotten inside. Wearing the cap backwards is even worse.

2. NEVER wear a winter hat or skull cap indoors and DEFINITELY never wear one during months when the weather is warm. Trust me, there is nothing more ignorant looking than a guy in a winter skull cap when it is 90 degrees outside.

3. Do not wear a lot of jewelry to class. I would hesitate to attend class wearing large earrings or any type of jewelry that brings attention.

4. Look at the other students in the class and take note of what they are wearing (or aren't wearing). Today's students admittedly don't "dress to impress" on campus like in the "old days," but my guess is that you won't see too many other male students who aren't of color wearing skull caps, big, cheap looking earrings or baggy jeans that are falling off in the classroom. And even if you do, you should still avoid those things at all costs.

Wearing proper clothing while on campus is only one way to combat negative stereotypes regarding African-American males, but it is important. While these things are popular today amongst many young African-American males (and some young white males as well), they aren't viewed positively on college campuses. Even if no one pulls you to the side to let you know, these things are unacceptable, especially in an academic setting. You will look unprofessional and you won't be taken seriously. And trust me, you DEFINITELY want to be taken seriously!

CHALLENGE: Today I challenge you to not allow your appearance to tell a story about you that is not true. You are a student, an athlete and a representative of your family. What you wear should always reflect that.

CHAPTER 11

ALEX "AT" TURNER –
"THE BUSINESS MOGUL"

Talented people hit targets no one else can hit. Ambitious people aim to hit targets no one else can SEE. – Adoo S. Mukhtar

Alex Turner – better known as AT – was the only one of DaFellaz that didn't play football. He actually decided to attend Vanderbilt because Derrick Payne (#24), his long-time best friend from his hometown Memphis, was going to Vandy to play football like the rest of us. AT and DPayne were inseparable since they'd met, so I'm not surprised they decided to attend the same college. Although he didn't play ball, like most of our crew, AT had a difficult time academically at Vanderbilt in the beginning. But he wasn't afraid of anyone and had a personality that made him as comfortable in his own skin as anyone I had ever encountered, especially considering that he was just 17 years old. Although he was the youngest the 11 of us, AT would talk to anyone, at any time about ANYTHING and I admired him for that.

AT was committed to one thing, mainly – making money (legally), something he had been doing before he ever set foot on Vandy's campus. He actually started his first business in the seventh grade when one of his uncles gave him a button maker. His classmates would give him different logos to put on the buttons and he would produce them, for a fee of course. In middle school he began designing license plates and T-shirts using the African national colors of red, black and green, something that exploded and became very popular throughout the country a few years later.

When AT got to Vanderbilt, one of the first things he noticed was that many of our peers came from wealthy families. During our first year on campus, AT convinced a classmate to invest in a T-shirt business that he started in his dorm room. Each week during the football season, he produced a T-shirt with a theme about the teams we were playing. And each week the T-shirts sold out. This only fed AT's growing desire to be a business owner. Not only was he a young successful entrepreneur, he also knew how to have a good time. We only won three games our freshman year, but AT would always be one of the first guys to celebrate, win or lose. After all, he was making money off those shirts well before the outcome of the games. AT wasn't just the life of the party, he WAS the party.

AT's other love in college besides making money and enjoying life to the fullest was our fraternity, Kappa Alpha Psi. AT never missed an opportunity to fellowship with the brothers and was heavily involved with anything related to the fraternity after he pledged. He was as serious about being a Kappa as he was about being a businessman. I can't count the number of times my phone would ring in the dorm room in the middle of the night or early morning and AT would be on the other line saying, "Yo, D.Gragg, come up to my room and have a drink with me man!" And even if it was 2 o'clock in the morning, he could convince me to do just that. And we'd stay up until dawn sometimes just talking about life and our plans to take over the world. But his drive to be a businessman finally became too strong for him to ignore, leading him to leave Vandy right before our senior year to pursue building a T-shirt business back in Memphis. Soon after leaving school he founded the Homeboy Shoppin'

Network Company and began selling T-shirts and other apparel full-time in a mall in Memphis. He also sold apparel at athletic games and other events.

Seeking to take his business to even greater heights at only 22 years old, AT actually went to the Champion sporting apparel office in Memphis unannounced and asked to speak with one of the executives there. At the time, Champion was a major player in the sports world, producing uniforms for some of the NFL and NBA teams and many college teams. AT wanted to talk to someone about how he could maybe partner with the company. After waiting for more than an hour, AT finally met with one of the executives for more than three hours. After the meeting the executive told him, "Son, there are two important things that you need to know. Number one, don't EVER interrupt me when I'm in a meeting again. Number two, come back tomorrow." Just like that AT was on his way to becoming a young millionaire.

Not too long after that, someone came up with the idea of having the elite football players from the historically black colleges and universities play in an all-star game at the end of the season, similar to other college all-star games like the Blue-Gray game and the Senior Bowl. This would give the players from lesser-known schools the opportunity to showcase their talent for NFL scouts. The game was to be played in Atlanta, which is why AT headed down to the city for business meetings about selling T-shirts and other apparel at the first-ever all-star game. He celebrated his 23rd birthday in Atlanta during the discussions. Not only was AT in position to be one of the vendors at the game, he was working on overseeing all apparel sales at the game. Unfortunately, AT's dream didn't come true because he was killed in a car accident in Atlanta a few days after his birthday.

Decades later, this tragedy remains something many of us still can't believe or process. He died just as he'd lived in his short 23 years of life: going hard, chasing his dreams, living life to the fullest the entire time. Everyone who has lost someone special, probably has the same thoughts I have about AT: I wonder what that guy would be if he were still with us today? My bet is that he would be right alongside the big-time moguls of our era, BET founder Bob Johnson, "Shark Tank's" Daymond John, who founded the successful FUBU clothing company, hip hop super powers/businessmen Sean "P. Diddy" Combs and Shawn "Jay-Z" Carter, and anyone else you can think of that made something big out of nothing at all. Now we all know why AT went so hard so fast. He only had a very limited amount of time to make big things happen. I thank God I got to know him. AT, rest in heaven my Brother…

CHALLENGE: Today I challenge you to think and dream BIG. My Brother AT certainly did and you should, too. You can truly do anything you set you want to do with your life. The only limitations you have are the ones you set for YOURSELF. Forget about limitations and think about POSSIBILITIES. Start now!

Alex Turner at fraternity function – Vanderbilt University

CHAPTER 12

A SETBACK CAN BE A MAJOR SET <u>UP</u> FOR BIG THINGS TO COME!

"Every setback is a setup for a comeback." – T.D. Jakes

No matter how good we are at doing something or how successful we may become, we all will experience major setbacks in life. Some of these setbacks are not nearly as bad after a while as we once thought, but some setbacks can be life-altering and devastating. The devastating setbacks are the ones that leave you feeling like you will never recover. Your girlfriend is dating someone you thought was your friend; you failed a class and are now on academic probation; you dropped the winning touchdown pass or missed the tying free throw in the last seconds of the game… It's easy for me to say that you should just shake these things off and move on, but I, myself, have experienced setbacks I did not think I could overcome. But, trust me, you can learn a LOT from a setback and be set UP for success in the future.

My first major setback in college occurred during my sophomore year during the fourth week of the football season. I had worked hard during the off-season and at the time, I was the starting wide receiver on the team. I was so proud and felt that my skills and talent on the field were validated, especially after only catching two passes my freshman year as a back-up to two very talented senior receivers. Our team was heading into our first conference game against the Florida Gators down in their home stadium, famously known as "The Swamp." On the Wednesday prior to the game,

my position coach called me into his office for a pep talk to reassure me that I was the "top guy" in my position and that I just needed to relax and go out and play. He told me that I was the top receiver on the team and that I was living up to the lofty reputation I brought with me as the top receiver recruit in our class. We were about to play a team whose defense was nationally ranked and sent several players to the NFL. And, oh, on offense they had Heisman Trophy candidate and future NFL Hall of Famer Emmitt Smith, who retired from the NFL as the all-time leading rusher in football history. Their team was "loaded,", so my coach's confidence in me made me feel good about facing one of the top teams in the country.

As expected, Florida blew us out of the stadium winning 34-11. Emmitt Smith had 202 yards on 25 carries (as I recall, Smith may have set a new school rushing record against us that day), and we went into the locker room at half time down 27-3. Like against most of the SEC teams we played during my four years at Vandy, we were overmatched on the field and coaching-wise. We simply could not keep up with the team that boasted the player who was named SEC Most Valuable Player after the season (Smith, who elected to go into the NFL draft instead of returning for his senior season at Florida, was drafted in the first round as the 17th pick overall. (Additionally, 20 of the players on Florida's team that day were drafted into the NFL during the next three years compared to the one or two who were drafted from our team).

The day after the game, we had our usual film study session to review the past day's game and work on correcting mistakes that been made in preparation for the next week's game. Again, my position coach called me into his office for a one-on-one meeting. However, his message time was

MUCH different than the pep talk he had given me just four days earlier. He told me that he and the head coach had decided I was no longer "the guy" at the wide receiver position, that I was actually the least productive player on the offense and they were benching me and moving me from the Number 1 player at that position to Number 3. I remember thinking to myself, "What happened to just going down to Number 2?" but I was too stunned to even respond. I actually thought that the coach was joking with me to see how I would react. However, it turned out that he was very serious; so serious, in fact, that I spent the last two and a half years of my career as the back-up receiver to one of my best friends and DaFellaz member Clarence "Money Hands" Sevillian who ended up ranked in the top 10 of all-time at Vandy during that time. (The competitor that I am does have to point out that after I was benched Clarence caught 21 passes that season and I caught 20, not bad for a "scrub back up player.")

As you can imagine, I was very angry when I received this news. I wanted to throw my playbook across the room and tell the coach exactly how I felt about not being given another chance to prove that I could play better. I also thought seriously about giving up, packing my bags and quitting. We had only won four of the sixteen games that first year and a half I was at Vandy, so who needed to be a part of such a sorry program? I wasn't a part of the defense that gave up all those yards to Emmitt Smith, a defense that was the worst defense in the entire nation the very next season. I felt that the coaches were not taking any responsibility for our team's status and that instead I was being blamed as the problem. I felt the "weight of the world" in that meeting that day and I obviously have never forgotten it. However, when I returned to my dorm room I quickly decided that no matter what, I was going to work hard and finish what I started. This was definitely a big setback for me, but I was determined to stay with the teammates I had grown to love as brothers during the past two years. When my playing days in college were over, the four teams I played on had a 10-34 record. We actually won five of those 10 games during my senior year after a coaching change was made and Gerry DiNardo was brought in after my junior year. "Coach D," as we call him, was named SEC Coach of the Year and went on to coach at LSU and Indiana. And DaFellaz went on to become one of the most prolific group of players in Vanderbilt football history both on and off the field.

This setback made me focus much more on my academics and I shifted my focus and priorities. No longer did I view football as my top priority. I began concentrating fully on academics and graduation and was named to the All-Academic SEC Team two years later. I also joined my fraternity and inherited another set of brothers and best friends for life who helped keep me focused on what was really important. There is no doubt in my mind that this set back is what laid the foundation for where I am today professionally. The setback brought on a reality I had not considered before: Football simply was not that important in the grand scheme of things then, or now. At the end of the day, my setback was a major set UP for me. A set up that has led to me becoming the youngest African-American athletic director in the country years later.

Just remember that whatever you are going through – struggling academically, injury, getting less playing time than the guy in front of you on the depth chart – it is not the end of the world, especially when you are YOUNG. Trust me, you will bounce back. I know it's tough now, but try to learn from your experience. Grow, mature and focus on the things you CAN control – work hard in the classroom, plan for the future, stay out of trouble and, ultimately, GRADUATE! Keep the situation from defining who you really are. Remember, sometimes bad things happen to very good people. Do not give up on your lifelong dreams. Keep moving forward, despite the problems or challenges you may face. Your setback can DEFINITELY be the major SET-UP for you and those around you!

CHALLENGE: Today I challenge you to focus on what is in front of you instead of what has happened to you in the past. You won't forget, but don't let what HAS happened define what lies ahead for you in life. Don't let the setbacks in life keep you from the great set-ups in store for you!

Dr. Derrick Gragg & Lovie Smith, University of Tulsa Alum and Head Coach of the Tampa Bay Buccaneers

CHAPTER 13

YOUR BOY: IT MAY BE TIME TO LET HIM GO

"Some relationships are designed to get you from A to B, not A to Z." - Dr. Derrick Gragg

Do you ever notice that when you got into serious trouble, nine times out of 10, one of your "boys" was with you? Or, even worse, one of your boys talked you into something you knew was wrong in the first place, and both – or all – of you ended up in big trouble? It may have started when you were in elementary school and your boy was the kid who got caught throwing rocks at other kids and at passing cars. In middle school, your boy discovered his mama's cigarettes and brought them to school to smoke. Of course, you joined in even though the smell of the smoke made you want to puke. And by high school, your boy had moved on from an occasional cigarette from mama's purse to beer, weed and driving recklessly through your neighborhood, even before he got his driver's license. This was also around the time when he started doing other illegal things that drew the attention of the school and police officers. And for some STRANGE reason, you were right there at his side through most of this foolishness. Luckily for you, HE has been the one who has gotten into most of the trouble. Trust me, if this guy were TRULY your boy, your ace, your "dog," then he we would never drag you into crazy situations which you have to ultimately explain to your coaches, parents and university administrators.

One of my boys in high school went on to college and coincidentally joined the same fraternity as I did. During the summers, we were inseparable when I went home to relax before football training started up again. He was always a bit mischievous when we were in high school, but I didn't think much of it. As we got a little older, I started hearing rumors about him, and how he got the sports car he started driving when we were in college. While I was home one summer, I was cruising through town with him trying to impress the young ladies. I remember we stopped at another frat brother's home to hang out for a little while and drink a beer or two. Suddenly, before I had even taken a sip of the beer, my boy's pager went off. He looked down at it quickly and said, "Hey man, we need to go, I have to make this run." My instincts told me that I should not go on that "run," so I convinced him to drop me off at another frat brother's apartment instead. I never saw him again after that because soon afterward, he was arrested, which turned out to be the first of several arrests for him. Unfortunately, he is now in prison serving a 30-plus year sentence.

I have some advice for you. The next time one of your boys wants you to do something that could cost you your opportunity to play ball, graduate from college and pursue the things you've always wanted, do this: Picture your mom's face when she comes to pick you up from school after you get expelled. Picture your grandmother when you have to tell her she won't be watching you on TV next weekend during the big game, because you will be at home sitting out the semester for doing things she told you repeatedly not to do as you were growing up. Or even worse, picture yourself in a 6- by-8-foot concrete cell where you live 20-plus hours a day. Remember, jails and prisons are full of people who are just like our boys.

CHALLENGE: Today I challenge you to push away from anyone who will lead you down a path of destruction, even if that person is your family member, best friend or your boy. Sometimes in life you will have to leave some people behind in order to get to where you want to go.

CHAPTER 14

THE UNDERACHIEVER – DON'T LET THIS BE <u>YOU</u>

The line between failure and success is so fine that we scarcely know when we pass it – so fine that we are often on the line and do not know it. How many a man has thrown up his hands at a time when a little more effort, a little more patience, would have achieved success? - Elbert Hubbard

Many years ago I was a young athletic administrator in an entry-level position at Vanderbilt University, my alma mater. I was one of the athletic department's first full-time, hands-on academic counselors. At 24 years old, I was only one year removed from being a Vanderbilt football player myself, so, I related well to the student-athletes I advised (and sometimes yelled at). The athletes respected me and my opinions, mainly because I had "been there and done that." I knew exactly what they faced while studying at one of the most academically-competitive universities in the world while competing in the Southeastern Conference, the toughest football conference in the nation.

Back then, I wrote the following letter to a young football player I was counseling. The letter reflected my frustration with the young man. He was bright, articulate and eminently capable of succeeding as a student at Vanderbilt. However, like so many other student-athletes who fail academically, he simply did not feel academics were as important as football. He bought into the stereotypes used to describe athletes (black athletes, in particular), and seemed determined to do everything he could to fail. The words in this letter are just as relevant today as they were when I wrote them many years ago.

Dear: (Name Withheld),

64

Have you ever heard anyone refer to another person as an "underachiever"? The dictionary describes an underachiever as "someone who fails to achieve his or her potential or does not do nearly as well as expected." I have reviewed your high school records and your academic records here, and I am disturbed by your academic progress thus far. To get directly to the point, there is no reason you should not be doing better in school. You have become an "underachiever" in academics. I am not pointing this out to just criticize you; I am simply pointing out the truth. You have hardly attended study table this semester, and you don't seem to care about bettering yourself academically. I know it doesn't seem important to you right now, but your academic record will follow you the rest of your life.

When you first got here, you struggled academically. That is not unusual. I, along with many other former student-athletes, struggled during our first year here. My first year GPA was probably worse than 95% of the students who attended this university. So, I definitely understand when student-

athletes struggle. But what I don't understand is the why you don't seem to care about school and whether you graduate or not. You don't care what your grades are just as long as you get by. Struggling is nothing to be ashamed of, but not caring about academics is.

Do you know how many people would do anything to be in your shoes? I wish I were a part of your team: a team that will change our program and go down in history. Wouldn't it be a shame if you were not here to enjoy all the success that is right around the corner? You know how important your education is to your mother. Wouldn't it be a total embarrassment to you and your family if you failed out of school? You, one of the most talented, gifted young men in your hometown, a college flunk-out. Why? Because you don't want to do what it takes to be successful. You don't want to study after practice because you are tired and your legs are sore. You don't want to get out of bed and go to practice because you stayed up all night with your girlfriend. You don't want to re-write your paper to get a better grade because you had a party to go to. So many excuses... I can see it all in the headlines in your hometown. What a shame. You have all that talent and you're blowing it, just trying to get by.

Don't go through life just getting by, <u>EXCEL</u>! Only those who excel will make it in life. I have seen a lot of young men like you come and go. Many graduated; some did not. Those who did not push themselves academically fell by the wayside as the program continued to move forward. I hope you don't let that happen to you. Most good jobs, with the exception of professional sports, require a person to have at least a bachelor's degree. I recently saw two of the past athletes who flunked out of school and told me that he wishes he could go back in time and talk to himself when he was here at this university. He said that he would warn himself about what he would face as an uneducated young man. He said that his lack of education led him into his current profession - dealing drugs. The other young man is back in his hometown, living in poverty and he has fathered at least four children. He was only 6 hours (2 classes) away from graduating. These are true stories.

When you leave this university, whether it be by graduation or failing out, you will be replaced. You must think about tomorrow, ten years from now and even twenty years down the road. You must think about your future.

So, you decide. The time has come for you to grow up and become responsible and take control of your life. If you don't, who will? There is only so much that I can say or do. Your life will change drastically over the next few years, and I hope that the changes will be positive ones. You probably will be done playing football forever, and you will be replaced as I once was. However, what you do here academically will be a permanent part of your life. My job is to monitor academic progress and make sure that you have all the necessary resources to strengthen yourself academically. I feel that I have delivered on my end of the bargain. The rest is up to you.

CHALLENGE: Don't ever become an underachiever. Today I challenge you to put forth as much effort inside the classroom as you do on the football field or court. Remember that your athletic career will end soon, but what you do in the classroom will last FOREVER.

CHAPTER 15

#88 JASON BROWN, WIDE RECEIVER – "THE MASTERMIND"

"We fall down sometimes. But we get back up again, because the ground is no place for a champion." – Rev. Jesse Jackson

Photo Credit: Vanderbilt Athletics

I first met Jason Brown ("Jay") during an orientation meeting for freshmen football players. Jay was a "walk-on" player, meaning that unlike the rest of us, he was not on football scholarship. He actually attended Vandy on an academic scholarship instead. Like the other first-year players, we were all excited because we would be the first class to "turn things around" for Vandy football and win the SEC championship (at least that was our goal). Those first days brought some very harsh realities. Pre-season workouts were much tougher than our previous high school days. The only thing that kept the other young guys and me from going insane was the fact that we had EACH OTHER. I remember thinking that I'd made a mistake by wanting to play college ball, especially since I'd turned down other opportunities go to college on an academic scholarship. Therefore, I couldn't understand why Jay wanted to play so badly, especially since he did not HAVE to be out there sweating and killing himself with those of us who were being "paid" to be there. I just could not understand a deep love for that type of mental and physical punishment, ESPECIALLY when there were so many other things he could be doing.

Since Jay and I were both wide receivers, we spent even more time together. One day after practice I approached him as he sat quietly in his locker with two big bags of ice on his ankles. "Man, for real, why in the WORLD are you doing this, Jay?" I asked him, "Don't you have an ACADEMIC scholarship? Man, we HAVE to be out here because we're on football scholarship. If I were you, I'd be in my dorm room studying or finding some ladies or something. If you lose your scholarship, how are you going to pay for school, dude? You'll have to go home!" I continued. What I didn't know about Jay at the time that I know very well now is that he LOVED the game and he loved us, DaFellaz, even more.

I remember the day Jay finally gave up on the college ball player dream. He was trying his hardest to catch passes during a spring football practice our freshman year. He ran a simple 10-yard out route, turned his head, and dived for a very catchable pass that hit both his hands. He fell face first into the turf and dropped the pass. He got up, glanced over at me and limped off the field. He didn't say anything at the time, but I could tell his career was over by the way he walked off the field. But I have always admired his relentless passion for the game and passion for the game and for being one of DaFellaz. Jay didn't make it on our team very long, but not because of his EFFORT.

The true tragedy at that time was that Jay's focus on football was a major distraction that took him away from his studies and his focus on what was paying his way to Vandy – his academic scholarship. Sadly, to avoid being kicked out of college after our sophomore year, Jay voluntarily withdrew from school. He moved back to his hometown of Brooklyn, New York, where he worked as a night janitor while attending a junior college. The bigger challenge was that he had also gotten his girlfriend in Nashville pregnant. When Jay decided to marry his girlfriend soon after his 22nd birthday, Carlos Thomas, another member of DaFellaz, jokingly labeled the Jay and his new wife, Felicia, "Most Unlikely to Succeed." But Jay's relentless spirit, passion for his family and for making something of himself have inspired me over the years.

Not only did Jay go on to graduate from St. John's University, he also earned an MBA at the same university. Jay is now the Executive Director, head of Global Communications Compliance at J.P. Morgan Assets Management, where he has worked for more than 10 years. He works in a high-rise building in New York City similar to the ones he had to clean up years ago to make it through junior college. And oh, yeah, he's been married to Felicia for the past 23 years and that baby they had in college just graduated from Penn State University. Jay is without a doubt one of the most successful businessmen in the country in his field. How is THAT for "Mr. Most Unlikely to Succeed?"

The main message I want to stress is that no matter what you pursue, GO HARD, be relentless and passionate about your goals. Like Jay and so many others, sometimes you may have to change your original plans and go in a different direction to make it. But whatever happens along the way, you have to keep pushing and moving forward. Remember my previous chapter: Sometimes setbacks can be major setups for success. Jay made it, and you will, too!

CHALLENGE: Today I challenge you to GO HARD and give everything you have to get where you are trying to go. You may have to take a different path at times, but do not stop! Life is made up of many, many changes. Adjust and keep pushing. My man Jay did it and so can you!

CHAPTER 16

JUST **DON'T** DO IT

"I'm accountable to you. What I put out on that football field today is not for me, it's for YOU. You will never be disappointed in me." — Michael Strahan, Hall of Fame induction speech

Every day it seems we hear a new story about something going wrong in college sports, especially in football or men's basketball. How many times have you heard about the kid who took money from a booster or an agent? How about the guys who are hitting women? And how about the guys who always seem to get into big fights at nightclubs and parties on and off campus?

The next time you're in a team meeting, look at the guy that's sitting right next to you. Unless the coaches have some type of special seating chart you're following, my guess is that you're sitting next to one of your closest friends on the team and on the entire campus. I have mentioned my former roommate, Corey Harris. From the first day we met until we graduated together four years later, we were inseparable. We sat with each other at every team meeting, rode the team bus together, ate lunch together on campus at the same time every day for four years, and traveled to each other's hometowns during breaks from school. And, when we were allowed to live off campus, we shared an apartment together along with our Fraternity Brother and DaFellaz member William Brown. Corey and I relied on one another and trusted each other COMPLETELY. We would never do anything to put our boys in a bad situation, even if we did something stupid on our own. And you should never put your boys, teammates or friends in bad situations either. As the title of this chapter reads: JUST DON'T DO IT.

If you find yourself in one of those situations where you have to make a hard decision, think about your boys who sit next to you at the team meetings. As someone who came up without the money and material things that many of my college classmates had, I definitely understand wanting to experience some of the "finer things in life." But you shouldn't take money or gifts from fans, boosters or friends of the program. You probably haven't ever heard of a positive story about an athlete who accepted gifts or money in college. Those situations usually end very badly for the athlete involved.

I know it's tough to always do the right thing, especially there are people out there who don't care about you and are jealous because you are a college baller. They look for opportunities to provoke you into fighting and more serious violence. But once you throw that punch, though, you alone will end up on the front page of the paper and the video of the fight (since EVERYTHING is taped these days) will go viral in a matter of minutes. You will be labeled as that "out of control ball player who doesn't belong on campus anyway." You could also lose your scholarship, be thrown out of school or go to jail.

So if you REALLY care about your guys, your teammates, you won't do anything to jeopardize all the hard work that all of you have put in to get you this far. And if you are willing to throw it all away for something that will be meaningless to you a few days, weeks or months from now, you shouldn't be on the team, anyway. JUST DON'T DO IT to yourself, your boys, or your team. At some point in your life, your reputation and good name are going to speak volumes about you, and people will listen closely to what your reputation says.

I'm not saying I was ever perfect, or that my teammates were "angels," but I do know we all looked out for each other. Even more than that, we looked out for OURSELVES. Isn't that what a teammate is supposed to do? So, be the designated driver. Or the one who helps your teammate calm down and walk away when he is arguing with his girl. You never know what a huge impact you can make just by making the right decision – or helping one of your boys to make the right decision, as well.

CHALLENGE: Today I challenge you to think more about the things you may be doing that affect your teammates, especially your very best friends on the team. Do not let them down (and don't let yourself down, either) by doing something that will destroy everything you've worked so hard for since we got where you are right now.

CHAPTER 17

THE "DUMB JOCK" MUST BE DESTROYED

"Education is the most powerful weapon you can use to change the world." — Nelson Mandela

When did it become really popular to be a "dumb jock" who ignores academics and doesn't take school seriously? Today, "smart" kids are sometimes harassed, made fun of and sometimes even physically threatened or abused because they make good grades and are academically talented. This is often true in the world of college athletics, particularly with regard to African-American athletes. Some modern-day African-American athletes are better compared to Roman gladiators who were admired solely for their physical strength and abilities, than to their African-American forefathers who epitomized the well-rounded scholar-athlete. But WHY is this happening? Well, it appears that some African-American students *intentionally* underachieve academically. Since some African-American students do not want to be singled out as smart or intelligent by their friends or teammates, they underachieve on purpose to gain acceptance from them. Other athletes simply do not try to do well academically because they have never done well in the classroom. They may have been passed along in school because they were good athletes or they may have learning disabilities that have never been addressed or corrected. And some simply don't care about school because they are too focused on becoming a star ball player who goes on to make millions in the league.

In any group or team setting, you will often be forced to come into contact with people who do not think the way you do or want to work as hard as you do to make something of themselves. PLEASE do not let them influence you! If you have to pretend to be dumb and fail academically to "fit in" with a group that is NOT the group for you! Find the members of your family, fraternity, or team who are POSITIVE and want to achieve in the classroom. I'm not asking you to be a brainiac or rocket scientist; I'm just asking that you work as hard in the classroom as you do on the field, court and track.

In addition to students intentionally failing to do well academically, anti-intellectualism (or "dumbing down and appearing to be unintelligent or just not caring anything about school) is often embedded deeply within the athletic culture. Dr. Harry Edwards, one of the most significant figures in sport history, once said that "dumb jocks are not born; they are systematically created," which means that student-athlete anti-intellectualism is a product of the athletic culture and environment, rather than solely a product of a student-athlete's own views and attitudes towards academics. Thus, the academic "gap" between student-athletes who underachieve academically and those who are more successful in the classroom is the product of low expectations of coaches, student-athlete academic advisors, and other students on campus, faculty, alumni, and the public rather than only a low level of academic ability.

Recently I ran into a former student-athlete at a reception who was exactly like the people I am describing in this chapter. He didn't care about academics at all and did not want to do anything other than play ball. As his academic counselor, I had to wake him up in study table and go find him on campus when he was late for academic appointments. Since he was a good player who was a four-year starter, he thought he was going to the

NBA for sure. Although he is one of his school's all-time greatest players, he was not drafted into the league and was a member of an NBA team for less than a week into the regular season before being cut. He never played in the NBA again. However, what makes me feel proud is that every time I see him, he tells anyone who is around us that I am the reason he graduated from college. He is now a successful high school coach himself.

Don't be fooled, you will definitely need an education to succeed in today's society. Even if you want to own your own business, you should enroll in a few business courses to learn as much as you can about being a business owner. Stop listening to people who aren't serious about academics, even if they are your best friends, family members, teammates, or others who are close to you. Those people are probably unsuccessful in life themselves, so you REALLY should not allow them to influence you.

CHALLENGE: Today I challenge you to do your VERY best academically and to work as hard as in the classroom as you do on the field or court. Being a dumb jock may be "cool" to some, but you should never feed into it. The quickest way to fail is to ignore the main focus of college – to get an education.

DaFellaz member Corey Harris with then Vanderbilt Chancellor Joe B. Wyatt prior to graduation ceremony

CHAPTER 18

#34 DR. CARLOS THOMAS, FULLBACK - "THE REVOLUTIONARY"

"The ultimate measure of a man is not where he stands in moments of comfort and convenience, but where he stands in times of challenge and controversy." - Dr. Martin Luther King, Jr.

Photo Credit: Vanderbilt Athletics

"Carlos!!!! Carlos!!!!" I couldn't believe my ears as we walked into our football stadium that afternoon. Here we were, about to defend the home turf against the University of Mississippi (Ole Miss) Rebels — who were ranked in the top 20 at the time — and our fans were being drowned out by the Ole Miss faithful who were yelling my best friend's name at the tops of their collective lungs. Of course if they had been yelling his name in support I would have felt much better. However, this was not a show of support or anything CLOSE to that.

"Carlos, we're gonna kick your ass today boy!" "The South will rise again Carlos boy!" "Hey Carlos, how do you like my flags?" one fan asked loudly as he waved a Confederate flag and hurled a Jack Daniels whiskey bottle he'd snuck into the stadium. There was violent tension in the air and the bottles were flying. Security actually had to be beefed up to protect us. Security beefed up to protect a football team in its *own stadium?*

Have you ever been around someone who you felt wasn't afraid of anything, was unafraid to speak his mind and stood strong in his opinions even if his opinions caused a controversy? Dr. Martin Luther King Jr., Nelson Mandela, Muhammed Ali, Michael Eric Dyson, Malcolm X, W.E.B. DuBois and others are just a few of the bold black men who have been outspoken, causing controversy and violent retaliation. They say what they want to say and stand by it no matter what. This is exactly how my best friend and teammate Carlos has always been. He stands up for what he feels is right, despite the consequences.

As Carlos now explains what happened, "Coming up to the incident that occurred with Ole Miss, we're talking about three years of racial and self-discovery, man. So, I was listening to (hip hop group) Public Enemy in high school and college and then I started taking African-American Studies classes at Vandy. I really started to question what the hell was going on around me – particularly as a student-athlete. I was always taught to be outspoken and to speak my mind."

Carlos continued, "Now, mind you, we were working on our second consecutive 1-10 season. And nobody is taking us seriously. So a reporter says, 'Well Carlos, you're from Memphis, were you recruited at Ole Miss?' I said, 'Yes, they recruited me.' So then he asked, 'So why didn't you go there?' That was my opportunity to really express myself, so I said, 'Because I could never play for a school that has the Confederate flag as its symbol.' Then the reporter asked, 'Carlos, did anyone do anything to you or say anything to you?' And I said, 'No, nobody did anything, I just couldn't play for a school that has the Confederate flag as its official or unofficial symbol.'

"Then he prodded me with a couple more questions and I said, 'Look Mr.___, I don't like Ole Miss, it's that simple. I don't even like the state of Mississippi!'

Carlos recalls, "So then, we have the game, and it was OUT OF CONTROL! It looked like millions of Confederate flags were flying that day IN OUR STADIUM. It was crazy! Everyone from Ole Miss calling my name! I remember leaving the field having Jack Daniels bottles thrown at us, Cokes, beer bottles and other things. They even beefed up security and I was receiving DEATH THREATS! I remember one teammate was mad at me because his brother played at Ole Miss. And his dad played there too I think. But I told him, 'Look man, that's just how black people feel about that flag!' You know, we were always taught to just keep our voices muted when it came to stuff that was remotely controversial because society didn't want to deal with the fact that you had these big brutes out there hitting each other, but they had intelligence."

I actually didn't blame Carlos for feeling the way he felt about Ole Miss and the Confederate flag. Neither did my black teammates. Many of us were born and raised in the South, and no matter how historians or others pointed to the Stars and Bars as a symbol of Southern pride, we viewed it as the supreme symbol of hate, bigotry and racism. As someone who grew up in Alabama, I myself can think of no more offensive American historical symbol.

During the past years, Carlos has earned not one, but TWO, doctoral degrees, has served as the Vice President for information technology at Southern University in Baton Rouge and is now the university's Director of the Student Innovation Collaboratory (SICL). Needless to say, I am VERY proud of Carlos for not only the things he has accomplished in life, but also for doing it while being HIMSELF, for standing up for what he feels is right. As I often say, "Be the same you that got you this far," something Carlos mastered a long time ago.

The tragic murders of nine African-American men and women at the historic Emanuel African Methodist Episcopal Church in Charleston, South Carolina – one of the oldest black churches in the country – fueled the growing controversy of the Confederate flag and its relevance in American society. The younger generation should know that this is a very old issue, one that's reared its ugly head before. Throughout history, African-Americans have generally labeled the Confederate flag as an offensive symbol of racism, oppression and violence.

Even a number of Southern politicians and business leaders, have begun to shift their views. Some have begun to take the strong stand against the Confederate flag, asking for it to be removed from state capitol grounds and other venues saying that the Confederate flag belongs in museums, not publicly displayed. I definitely agree. Carlos basically said the exact same thing 25 years ago. I applaud Ole Miss's leadership, alumni and fans' efforts to replace the Confederate flags with the "M" flags that have flown at football games since the late 1990's. I also applaud the leaders of South Carolina who voted to have the Confederate flag removed from the state capitol grounds. I know these were difficult cultural changes for some to make, but changes that were very critical and necessary.

CHALLENGE: Today, I challenge you to stick to your convictions and stand up for what you believe is right. Of course, you should never be reckless and do things that could ruin your future. But you will find that some things in life are worth taking a stance. STAND UP!

CHAPTER 19

STAY TRUE TO YOURSELF

**"I'd rather be hated on for who I am, than to be loved for who I'm not" –
Anderson .Paak (lyrics from "Medicine Man" by Dr. Dre)**

As a former student-athlete, I feel that one of my major strengths is being able to connect with current student-athletes. I always welcome the opportunity to meet with them in order learn what is on their minds. Sometimes, I am forced to have meetings that are more disciplinary in nature. One day, however, the head coach asked that I meet with a young man as a sort of intervention. The young man was a very talented and gifted athlete on the football field, and, according to his coaches, had the ability to become the most dominant player at his position in the entire conference. The coach was obviously frustrated with the young man because of his self-destructive behavior, such as skipping class and testing positive for marijuana. Like many college students away from home for the first time, the young man had picked up bad habits and hung with people who caused him to lose focus on the classroom and, ultimately, caused poor performance on the football field.

During my conversation with the young man, I learned more and more things that changed my perception of him. He wasn't the thuggish, undereducated person he portrayed, he was actually the son of a Southern Baptist minister. He was brought up in two-parent household where he was definitely taught right from wrong. But now he was losing his way and forgetting who he REALLY was and how he was raised. After speaking to him for a few minutes and hearing him talk more about his family background and upbringing, my message to the young man was simple: Don't try to be someone you aren't in order to fit in with someone you aren't like. Stop compromising yourself, your values, and your family's good name to be with people who aren't like you. If you compromise yourself now, you will continue to do it throughout life.

In his smash hit, "Public Service Announcement" hip hop legend Jay-Z says "You was who you was 'fore you got here," which means that, despite what successes or fame you may have in life, you are still the same person you were BEFORE the success came. On the flip side, you are also the same person you were before adversity and hard times or even some failures came your way. You should never compromise who you REALLY are, whether you are going through good times or bad times.

People who know me often hear me refer to myself as a "poor country boy from Alabama who did what his Mama told him to do; went to school and tried to stay out of trouble." That describes me in a nutshell. Despite the fancy "Dr." title in front of my name, the numerous committees I have served on throughout my career, the influential people I know and the great places I have been, I will always be that poor boy who grew up in a small home in Huntsville, Alabama who listened to his wise mother – PERIOD. That is my foundation. I can only be who I was before I got here and that is enough for me.

So many times as young people, we lose ourselves and drift away from our roots. As you continue to grow and mature, you will realize that life is a lot simpler when you go through it being YOU. After all, being you got you this far, right?

CHALLENGE: Today I challenge you to take a look in the mirror and remember who you **REALLY** are and what you stand for. Do not pretend to be someone else. Be **YOU**, the same you that got you this far.

CHAPTER 20

APPRECIATE GOOD FRIENDS - YOU CAN'T REPLACE THEM

"Remember, tomorrow is promised to no one." – Walter Payton

When you lose a best friend, it's often easy to remember the last time you saw that person alive. Although it was more than 20 years ago, I remember the last time I saw my man Alex (AT) like it was yesterday. I was playing a game of "noon hoops" with a few athletic co-workers. I often worked out to ease the stress of my everyday life of that time. I was 23 years old, married to my high school sweetheart, and my one-week old baby girl was in the Vanderbilt Hospital lying in an incubator fighting for her life. She was born nearly three months prematurely and the doctors only gave her a 20 percent chance of survival. I spent many hours outside of work at the hospital during the six weeks she was being cared for there. On that day, however, I was in need of a basketball stress-reliever.

Because I had not worked out since my daughter's birth, I wanted to get in a few extra minutes on the court before taking a break. On a trip down the court after our team scored a basket, I heard my man AT yell out to me. I was surprised because I had no idea he was even in town. AT lived back in his hometown of Memphis at the time, and I knew that he was working on some type of big business deal down in Atlanta. So he stopped mid-way in Nashville to check up on me before he met D. Payne across town where they talked and prayed together before AT hit the road.

"AT, give me a couple of minutes!" I said as I ran past him. After a couple of trips back down the floor I asked one of my teammates to sub for me so that I could go talk to him. In grand AT fashion, though, he had disappeared just as quickly as he had appeared. He was always on the go, so I didn't really think that much about it. I simply said to myself that I'd see him when he came back through town, like I always did. Little did I know, that was the last time I'd see AT alive...

About a week later, I was at the hospital visiting my daughter when I got a frantic call from another friend to tell me what had happened to AT. Bad car accident in Atlanta... Ran off the road... Died on the way to the hospital... This news stopped me in my tracks... The only positive part about all of this was that AT had no alcohol or drugs in his system when he passed. All of us who knew AT knew that he could drink, party and stay up late with the best of them, but he was always on another level when it came to handling business and making money. He wasn't down in Atlanta to party, he was there to continue his climb to become one of the youngest and richest entrepreneurs in the country. And I know he would have surely accomplished his goal. As you can imagine, even today I still regret not simply running off the court to at least shake his hand, give him the brotherly hugs we shared and a signature "Da Fellaz" kiss on the cheek in the style of those Magic Johnson and Isiah Thomas gave each other on the basketball court (proving that "bad boys" can be gentlemen, too). Through the years, I have replayed the last time I saw AT over and over in my mind. What I have come to realize is that he was actually there to tell me goodbye before he ventured to Atlanta to meet the fate the Lord had for him. I still wish that I had taken just ONE minute to slow down to give him that big brotherly hug and tell him that I loved him just one more time. Rest in peace, AT. You are sorely missed, my Brother.

CHALLENGE: Today I challenge you to drop your "manly guard" for a few minutes and tell you closest friends – your boys, your dogs, your aces - that you love them. Trust me, you will never regret saying it. I guarantee it.

Dr. Derrick Payne, Derrick's cousin Willie Armstrong and Alex Turner at Hamilton High School Graduation, 1988.

CHAPTER 21

#22 COREY HARRIS, TAILBACK - "THE CHAMPION"

"Losers quit when they're tired. Winners quit when they've WON." – Unknown

"A champion is someone who gets up when he can't." – Jack Dempsey, former heavy weight boxing World champion

Corey Harris as a Baltimore Raven - Photo Credit: *Baltimore Sun*

The first word that comes to mind when I think of my former roommate Corey "Snake" Harris is CHAMPION. Not only was Corey the most athletically-gifted guy I ever played with, he had a competitive spirit that matched his God-given talent. A lot of ball players have talent, but the ones who are the most competitive, work the hardest in practice, in the weight room during the off-season and never ever think they can be beaten are the ones who will become champions.

I remember watching Corey in drills our first day of freshman-only workouts and marveling how athletic he was. I remember watching his feet move at a pace that mine could not match during one of our drills and thinking to myself, "Man, THIS guy is different from the rest of us." And he was...Nothing was going to stop Corey from becoming a professional football player. He was so consumed with being a top-notch player that he considered leaving all of us at Vandy and transferring to another school to put himself in a better position to be noticed. I remember him talking seriously about transferring to Auburn, a school known for its superior running backs like Heisman Trophy winning "super back" Bo Jackson. Corey was tired of getting beaten up, tired of not getting the ball enough, and definitely tired of having to play positions other than running back. Corey had pattered himself after his idol, the great NFL Hall of Famer Eric Dickerson, but he was not getting the ball nearly as much as we needed him to be successful. He was just sick and tired of losing and could not accept it.

Fortunately for us, Corey stayed and ended up being named to the All SEC first team and Birmingham Football Club "Back of the Year" our senior year. He was the second player the Houston Oilers (now the Tennessee Titans) drafted that year as well. He was on his way, or so we THOUGHT. Although the Oilers had taken him very high in the draft they eventually cut him from the team during the fifth week of the season. I'll never forget seeing his name in the transaction section of the newspaper, which stated that he has been released. I immediately went to the nearest pay phone to call him (no one I knew owned a cell or i-Phone then).

"Man, what HAPPENED?" I asked him. I can't remember exactly what he said, but he told me to hold on because another call had come in on the other line. When he clicked back over to talk to me he said, "Hey man, I have to get to the airport in 45 minutes so I can catch a flight. Green Bay just picked me up!" Again, he was "on his way." Corey jumped on that plane to become a Green Bay Packer and never looked back. He ended up playing for an astonishing 12 years in the league with 6 different teams (remember, the average player only makes it 3-4 years) and became a Super Bowl champion as a member of the record-setting defensive unit for the Baltimore Ravens in 2001. That unit was led by a much younger future Hall of Famer Ray Lewis at the time. Corey also played with Hall of Famers Rod Woodson, Shannon Sharpe and Jonathan Ogden.

What I want to stress here is that Corey always surrounded himself with the best because he wanted to BE the best. Not only was he blessed with physical talent, he also worked longer and harder than everyone else. If you want to be the best, you can't surround yourself or hang out with

people who aren't at least TRYING to be the best themselves. You can't surround yourself with the worst people – those who are unmotivated, lazy, non-hustling or full of excuses and complaints – and be the best. Who are you surrounding yourself with?

NFL.com lists Corey as one of the top 10 all-time NFL players from Vanderbilt, ranking him #7 (of course I rank him higher than that). And although he never accomplished his goal of being named NFL Special Teams Player of the Year and will not make the NFL Hall of Fame like some of his former teammates, he is truly a CHAMPION.

Always remember that you can still win even if you fall short of your ultimate goals. You also may have to CHANGE and ADAPT in order to become successful. A great example of adapting is even though Corey was the most prolific running back in Vanderbilt history, he played two of his 12 of his years in the NFL on offense and the remaining 10 years as a DEFENSIVE BACK. He changed, adapted and did what he had to do to win. Are you willing to change? Are you willing to adapt? Do you REALLY want to be a champion?

Even today, Corey never stops thinking and dreaming. His energy is contagious and I am glad that he continues to inspire the young ball players he mentors who want to follow in his footsteps. You should also strive to become the CHAMPION that he has been his entire life.

CHALLENGE: Today, I challenge you to take your God-given talent to the next level by developing a "can't lose" attitude, eliminating distractions that do not make you better, and simply out-working everyone around you. Think, act and play like the CHAMPION you are!

Corey Harris, Dr. Derrick Payne, Marcus Wilson & Jason Brown
Photo Credit: Embrick Johnson

CHAPTER 22

DON'T FORGET THAT YOU CAME TO COLLEGE TO <u>GRADUATE</u>!

"Keep believing in yourself. Every goal that has ever been reached began with just one step – and the belief that it could be attained." – Jason Blume

Dr. Derrick Gragg - Doctoral Degree Photo, University of Arkansas

Simply put, you should do everything in your power to earn a college degree, period. Today with unemployment rising and blue-collar opportunities of yesterday drying up all across the country, if you do not graduate you greatly lower your chances of making things better for yourself and your family. As I have said over and over within these chapters, you simply cannot pin all your hopes and dreams on playing in the NFL or NBA. As a matter of fact, it would be VERY foolish to pin all your hopes to anything that can end so suddenly. Even if you are one of

94

the very few fortunate enough to play professional football, chances are that you will not play longer than three or four seasons. And, if you are unconvinced that college is important, I encourage you to watch the ESPN 30 for 30 film entitled "Broke" which lays out how very easily and quickly superstar athletes can lose millions and millions of dollars and have nothing left to show for the money they earned, not even the 10 expensive cars, houses or jewelry that they bought for themselves, their families and their boys.

Trust that I know how hard it is to focus and study when you're dead tired after classes, practicing and competing or traveling. I've been there. My "Talented Ten" boys DaFellaz have been there too. We know that there is nothing worse than attending study hall after long, hard (and often boring) practices. However, if you use your educational resources and develop yourself completely as a person, you can certainly graduate from college. Many universities and their athletic departments make millions of dollars during your years on campus. Therefore, make sure you leave school with something that can never be taken away – a sound education. Football, basketball, cars, clothes, jewelry and even relationships can disappear at any moment, but a college degree lasts forever. You aren't trying to just GET into college, the key is to FINISH college. Remember how hard you worked on the field or the court to get noticed to get here? That's the same way you have to work to graduate.

Always remember is that one of the easiest things for a black man to do in America is to FAIL. You must do whatever you can to keep from falling into what I call the "failure trap." You must continue to push hard, keep moving ahead and never, ever, give up! Work hard so you do not become one of the 94 young black men out of 100 who will never graduate from college. As you may have heard, college will be the best four or five years of your life. You will make your lifelong friends in college and may even find a partner to spend your life with. You should enjoy yourself and begin find out who you really are in college as well. But while you make those friends, and create those unforgettable memories never forget this: The number one reason you came to college is to graduate.

CHALLENGE: Today, I challenge you to finish what you started – GRADUATE! You are not on campus to be a ball player only. You have an opportunity to do something that many people can only dream about. Completing college should always be your top priority not your "back up plan." GO GET IT!

CHAPTER 23

WOMEN: OUR GREATEST DISTRACTION

"Women are like stars… Only one can make your dreams come true." – Unknown

In some of the other chapters of this book, I discuss some of the distractions that often lead us down the wrong path and keep people from becoming successful. I include women as a major distraction for men, but I realize that women are also very stabilizing forces in our lives and are often the backbone of their families. So this certainly isn't a chapter to bash women. I myself have some AMAZING women who have been part of my past and present lives. My mother is still my hero. My wife is another amazing woman who helped me put the pieces of my life back together when we began dating. I have a brilliant adult daughter who is finding her way through the maze of young life. I also have a fiery younger daughter (the baby of the family). I love all of the women in my life, but I have found that maintaining my relationships with them can be more than challenging. Therefore, I do not think that I am overstating things or exaggerating when I say that a female is oftentimes a man's greatest distraction.

The first rule for guys to remember is that even though we may pretend to be "all-knowing" about the opposite sex, we really don't know much about women at all. Even Steve Harvey, famed comedian, television star and author who has written two popular books about male-female relationships, says he is no expert on women. Quite honestly, I don't think any man is an actual expert on women. So, give it up men, you are NOT going to ever – EVER — figure out what makes a woman tick completely.

You may come close at some point after several experiences and relationships, but you DEFINITELY won't figure any of them out while you're 20 years old (and probably not when you're 30 or 40 either).

Also men — young men in particular — are sometimes taught by other men, television and now the Internet to "conquer" and "collect" as many females as possible. Trust me, this is a big mistake on many levels. I am certainly no expert on women, but I will offer you some great advice: If you want to cut down on the distractions and complications in your life, instead of "collecting" as many females as possible, you should instead limit the number of women/girls who are around you. Don't try to "juggle" or date a lot of women at the same time. As I tell my sons, focus on only ONE girl at the time. Society, images on television and in music and even your own boys may be telling you to be a "player," but wise, mature men will tell you that trying to have a "team" of women will lead to big-time distraction and disaster. And, when you are distracted, you cannot focus on what is most important right now: school, ball, working out, connecting with people on campus who aren't ball players, your coaches, making better grades and an overall positive college experience. You should also know that too many distractions can definitely affect your performance on the field or court – and not in a good way.

Again, I am definitely not being negative towards women; I'm just trying to give the guys reading this at least a CHANCE to limit their distractions. If you already don't understand women, why in the world would you try to "collect" and/or conquer so many of them? You already have several women who are "built into" your life: your mother, grandmothers, possibly a sister or two or more, your mother's sister or sisters, or her best friends or sorority sisters who still keep in touch with her etc. And then each of the women you have built into your life all have other women attached to them.

You need to make sure the women in your life are positive and guide you in the right direction. Women who "push your buttons," make you angry or persuade you to do anything that won't help you become a better person, graduate from college keep you out of trouble MUST be avoided. Love, commitment, trust, truth, honesty… WHOA… Once you grasp those words, you are ready to at least try to get into a serious relationship with ONE woman. Until then, you should always respect women and treat them the way you want men to treat your mother, sisters or aunts.

CHALLENGE: Today I challenge you to limit the number of women in your inner circle and focus on the ones who are most important. Don't buy into the "player" mentality. Always remember that you MUST respect ALL women you encounter at ALL TIMES.

CHAPTER 24

MOVIES, DOCUMENTARIES & BOOKS: YOU CAN LEARN SOMETHING FROM THEM

"Know a lot about a lot of things." Dr. G. Rankin Cooter

Due to all the changes in technology some say that books are less important now compared to when I was growing up. When I was young, I enjoyed visiting the public library and gathering as many books as I could to browse through, look at and check out to take home. As I grew older, my love for the library continued as I began to also fall in love with the mega bookstores Barnes and Noble and Borders. Today, the Internet, iPhones, iPads, tablets and computers have taken things to another level but the last comprehensive survey of public libraries showed that library usage is up, especially in children's materials – a very good thing. Although the amount of information these days can be overwhelming at times, you should take full advantage of the knowledge that is available to you.

My challenge to you is to do more than just read and watch television, movies or Internet shows to just be entertained. You should also try getting as much out of these experiences as possible. Below is a reference list of some favorite movies, documentaries and books that are more than simply entertaining; they will make you think and take a deeper look at yourself, where you came from and who you really are.

1. "Broke" - ESPN 30 for 30 documentary on former professional athletes' financial struggles
2. "American Paradox: Young Black Men" – Book written by Dr. Renford Reese, former Vanderbilt football star

3. "The Color Orange" – Documentary on former Tennessee quarterback Condredge Holloway

4. "Undefeated" – Documentary on an inner-city Memphis high school football team

5. "Crash" – Movie about racial tension and human problems in Los Angeles

6. "Higher Learning" – Movie directed by John Singleton (Boyz in the Hood) about racial and sexual identity and conflict in college, starring Ice Cube and Laurence Fishburne

7. "I am Ali" – In-depth look at the legendary Muhammed Ali that includes Ali's personal audio recordings

8. "Hip Hop: Beyond Beats and Rhymes" – Documentary highlighting the negative effects of hip hop music where several hip hop artists are interviewed

9. "Do the Right Thing" – Groundbreaking Oscar-nominated movie on race directed by filmmaker and outspoken activist Spike Lee

10. "The Express" – The story of Ernie Davis, the first black Heisman Trophy winner

11. "Kobe Bryant's Muse" – Biographical documentary about the superstar's life, career and challenges

12. "4 Little Girls" – Documentary about the 1963 16th Street Birmingham church bombing that killed four young black girls

13. "Iverson" – Showtime documentary on cultural icon and former NBA star Allen Iverson

14. "Remember the Titans" – Movie about the first African-American high school coach of a recently desegregated high school team in the state of Virginia

15. "Youngstown Boys" – ESPN 30 for 30 documentary on former Ohio State football star Maurice Clarett and former head coach Jim Tressel

16. "Say it Loud: An Illustrated History of the Black Athlete"

17. "The Pursuit of Happyness" – Movie starring Will Smith about Chris Gardner, formerly a homeless man who ends up founding his own multi-million dollar company

18. "History of the Civil Rights Movement" – CNN documentary

19. "Malcolm X" – Movie detailing the life of civil rights icon Malcolm X; directed by legendary film director/producer Spike Lee

20. "Dear White People" – Movie about black students attending a white college

21. "New Jim Crow: Mass Incarceration in the Age of Colorblindness" – Book analyzing the U.S. prison system and African-American males

22. "Jim Brown: All-American" – Documentary about the life NFL Hall of Famer Jim Brown

23. "Love and Basketball" – Movie about two long-time friends who fall in love while pursuing basketball careers

24. "Without Bias" – ESPN 30 for 30 documentary about the life and drug overdose death of University of Maryland basketball star Len Bias the night he was drafted by the Boston Celtics

25. "Quiet Strength" – Written by Tony Dungy, the first African-American NFL head coach to win the Super Bowl

26. President Barack Obama's autobiography that will be written and released after he leaves the White House

Of course, this list is far from being all-inclusive, but this will give you a great start on learning more about some of the inspirational people of color who have overcome great obstacles in life (some of the same things you may have overcome yourself) to achieve great things on and off the fields and courts of play. You will also witness how some people cannot overcome obstacles and instead are "swallowed up" by their circumstances and are doomed to failure. These aren't all "feel good" stories, but they all display life lessons you and others can learn from as you move toward your own life goals. Challenge yourself. Don't just watch TV and the movies. You can learn a lot by paying attention. Watch and LEARN…

CHALLENGE: Today I challenge you to learn something when you watch television or movies rather than just watching to be entertained. While there is nothing wrong with watching shows or movies that are enjoyable that may have no true message, don't limit yourself to just what entertains you. Always look to broaden your views and knowledge when you can. Start with this list and continue to add other movies, books or articles that can help educate you on as many topics as possible.

CHAPTER 25

USE IT OR LOSE IT!

"We ask ourselves, who am I to be brilliant, gorgeous, talented, and fabulous? Actually, who are you not to be? You are a child of God. Your playing "small" doesn't serve the world." – Nelson Mandela

During a recent visit with my family in my hometown of Huntsville, Alabama, I was able to connect with one of my best friends of the past 30 years. We met in high school in the ninth grade and were pretty much inseparable during our four years together there. However, as with many people, when I went off to college she and I didn't communicate as much. Even so, we always shared a very special bond that has lasted throughout bad marriages, divorces, second marriages, the deaths of parents, seven children between the two of us, and any and everything in between. It is always good to spend time with her and her family.

All three of my friend's children are honor stuents. Her two boys are going to be superstars on the baseball diamond/basketball court, and her daughter is a talented dancer. My friend is a very gifted singer, but none of her three children are as musically inclined as she is. During this particular visit to her home, she asked my youngest son, who is very musically-talented, to play her piano. She was looking for a "kindred spirit" of sorts to play some music for her. My son has literally been singing and dancing before the age of one and before he could even walk. He usually wakes us up each morning singing and has taken piano and voice lessons for years. My wife and I were very disappointed when he refused to play. After some time passed, my friend's husband pulled my son to the side to talk to him one-on-one.

"Son," he began, "You should never be afraid to share the talent you have with other people. Everyone usually has a special talent that not many other people have, so you have to make sure that your talent is known by everyone around you. God didn't bless you with a talent that He wouldn't want you to share with others around you."

I learned a very important lesson that evening just by listening. I agreed completely with what my friend's husband told my son. We should never been too shy, too bashful, too tired, or too whatever else to share the gifts we have received from God with other people. We should never be that selfish. You should display your talent as much and as often as you can, especially in a positive manner. If you are a writer, write! If you are a singer, sing! If you are a dancer, dance! If you are a great storyteller, tell great stories!

God has blessed us all with a special talent. Some of us are multi-talented. At some point, God may take those gifts from you, especially if you are athletically-gifted. Think about it; even the greatest athletes retire at some point and do not run, jump or move as easily or as gracefully as they once did. As I mentioned in a previous chapter, all athletes must eventually Retire, whether it is after high school, college, or the professional leagues, no matter how talented they are. The same is true of most professions. Make sure you don't let your talent go to waste. Share it with the world before it is too late!

CHALLENGE: God didn't give you all that talent so you could keep it all to yourself. Today I challenge you to tap into the talents others may not know you have. Begin to share your talents with those around you.

CHAPTER 26

#76 OSCAR MALONE III, DEFENSIVE TACKLE - "THE VISIONARY"

"No matter who you are, what you look like, where you come from, you can make it. That's an essential promise of America. Where you start should not determine where you end up." – President Barack Obama

Photo Credit: Vanderbilt University Athletics

Oscar Lee Malone III – or "Big-O" as we call him – is an amazingly talented individual who was a big-time ball player and is one of the most intelligent people I have ever met. He also has a sense of humor that rivals the great comics of today like Kevin Hart and Dave Chappelle. Although Big-O was 18 years old like the rest of us, he was already a "wise old man" who'd seen and been involved in things that some of us could not understand at the time. Big-O was an "Old Soul" who, rather than blast the hip hop of N.W.A, Public Enemy or the New Jack Swing of Bobby Brown, preferred the classic "Old School" R&B of Marvin Gaye, Al Green and Donny Hathaway. He was talented, funny, smart and mean as hell as a 300-pound defensive tackle. How could this guy lose? Like several of us, Big-O was a very highly recruited player who every college in the South wanted - especially the Miami Hurricanes, the biggest and "baddest" program of them all in our day. He had NFL success story written all over him.

Memphis has always been considered a "hotbed" for big-time football and basketball recruits and Big-O was among the most highly regarded recruits during his senior year. I honestly feel he made a big mistake by coming to Vandy rather than going to the University of Miami, better known as "The U." Like Vandy, Miami is a small, private school that competes in one of the best college sports conferences in the country. He could have gotten a great education at Miami and would have had a better chance of fulfilling his dreams of becoming a pro ball player. When we were in school, Miami was the "Bad Boys of College Football," as the media called them, and the most successful program in the country. Their players were cocky, brash, talked a lot – and backed it all up. Between 1985 and 1994, the Hurricanes won an NCAA record 58 straight home games. In 1986 and 1987, they went undefeated in the regular season, lost in the national championship game in 1986 and won national championships in 1987, 1989 and 1991.

Had Big-O gone to Miami he would have been on national championship teams in 1989 and 1991 and would have been 44-4 overall during his four years at The U. Four future NFL Hall of Famers played there during that time. Whoa... Vanderbilt's football program has come a very long way since we played there from 1988-92. During my four years, we only won 10 games TOTAL (Miami's yearly win average was even 11) and we won five of those 10 games during my senior year alone.

Out of the 11 of us, only William made decent grades our first year at Vanderbilt and Big-O definitely didn't adjust to the culture shock. Simply put, Big-O was pissed and frustrated, and it showed. He'd rebel in his own way. Even though he was as smart as anyone else in our class, he gave up academically. He'd go for days without attending class, staying up late and hanging with the older players. But he was still the only freshman to play in every game during our first year. Looking back, it is amazing that a guy who was so highly respected and well-educated today would not go to class or interact with anyone on campus who wasn't a ball player. He simply didn't care and his grades suffered because of it. And when he did decide that he really wanted to be there, it was too late. Like our boy Jay, after fighting academic probation, he was finally on his way out and for good.

What I have learned most from Big-O over the years is how to deal with hard times and overcome adversity. If anyone was supposed to fail it was him. He was a poor kid from the rough side of a rough inner city. He was SUPPOSED to lose at life. But like all the great success story-type people, Big-O did what he had to do, got back in school and not only graduated from The University of Memphis, he also graduated from law school there. His persistence has certainly paid off. The moral of this story is that your life may take many twists and turns as you continue to progress, but you should not allow circumstances, and especially other people to keep you from PERSISTENTLY pursuing what makes you happy in life. And even if you fail, remember that the most disappointing people are not the ones who pursue their goals with a passion and come up short, but those who never try to reach their goals at all.

I do think Big-O should have headed down to sunny Miami, The Land of the Hurricanes; but of course, we never would have met him. Without his presence early on, I do not think that we would have all been this close today. Actually, it was Big-O's naming us "DaFellaz" that bonded us even closer. We weren't like the wealthy privileged kids on campus, but we still had our own identity outside of just being ball players. We had an exclusive "club" that was our own. We were, and will forever be, DAFELLAZ and we owe that to Big-O.

CHALLENGE: Today, I challenge you to become even more serious about what you want to do in life. No one said that life was easy or fair. But you are a WINNER! Fight through it and carry on NO MATTER WHAT!

CHAPTER 27

IT COULD ALL END TODAY, SO STOP TAKING THINGS FOR GRANTED!

"Appreciate what you have before it turns into what you HAD." - Unknown

My oldest son Avery is probably one of the biggest sports fans of his age in the country. How could he NOT be, since he followed me from game to game around the country his entire life? Although I see many similarities in the two of us, I can honestly say that he loves football even more than I do - something I never thought possible. He has played for an organized football league every year since he was 8 years old. He seems to actually enjoy the tough workouts and other hard things one has to do to "shine" on the field. He never complains about how tough things are or how much time it takes to get better (unlike how his Old Man did during his ball-playing days). However, despite his love and passion for the game, he went through a life-altering situation that nearly ended his high school football career before it all began.

Everything in my son's life changed when he and his classmates returned from an eighth-grade field trip to Washington, D.C. Since they were scheduled to arrive back at the school around 6 a.m. after driving overnight, I was assigned to pick him up. The bus ride to and from D.C. was more than 10 hours long and my son and his friends emerged from the bus groggy and hungry. However, something else was also affecting my son. He could not hear out of his right ear. Over the next weeks, my son was analyzed by several hearing specialists and underwent a battery of hearing tests, but the doctors were (and still are) "stumped" regarding his hearing loss. We were told that the hearing in his ear was down to only 30 percent to 40 percent, at the most. One doctor also delivered the most crushing news of all: He could never play football or any other contact sport for the rest of his life. As you can imagine, the next hours and days were filled with sadness. Like many of you reading this, my son had put in countless hours practicing and playing the game he loved. And now all of a sudden, at 14 years old, it was all over. No more football. No following in his dad's footsteps as a scholarship athlete in college. No more chasing the dream.

Fortunately for Avery, we were blessed to have access to some of the best doctors in the region, and he was examined by several specialists after he was told he could no longer play. We kept praying and searching for a miracle. A few weeks later, on the first day of football practice at his high school, my son had an appointment with another doctor, who is actually one of the top specialists in the. Miraculously, my son was told that he

could play ball even though his hearing loss in his right ear might possibly be permanent. After discussing things with the doctor further just to make sure, I took Avery directly from the doctor's office directly to that first high school football practice. Due to the doctor's visit, he missed the first few minutes, but I will never ever forget how I felt when he jumped out of the car and ran across the field to join his teammates and coaches.

Many times, stories like this do not have such a happy ending. My son went on to fulfill a lifelong dream of playing college football, but he may never hear much out of that ear again. Although you've heard this saying a million times, you should always remember that it only takes one second, one play, to end your entire athletic career. When you are young, it is hard to understand just how blessed you are, whether you are an athlete or not. During the past 20-plus years working in athletics, I have seen college athletes' careers end in the blink of an eye. I want you to stop taking your life for granted, because it can all change very quickly.

CHALLENGE: Today I challenge you to stop taking life for granted. As the saying goes: Each day is a gift, that's why it's called the PRESENT. Live today like there is no tomorrow.

Avery Gragg as a high school junior football student-athlete

CHAPTER 28

SOCIAL MEDIA IS NOT ALWAYS YOUR FRIEND

"The Internet is not written in pencil ... it's written in ink." – *The Social Network* **movie**

Have you ever said something you immediately regretted saying? Something that made you wince or cringe? Something you wanted to take back right after you said it? Sure you have. We ALL have at one time or another in our lifetimes. Today, many people tend to communicate much more often through writing texts or emails and using other social media networks like Facebook, Instagram and twitter than they would at calling someone on the phone or writing a letter. As technology and communication through the Internet has literally exploded during the past few years, I have attempted to educate student-athletes about the problems they can cause themselves by making reckless comments on Twitter or posting inappropriate photos and comments on Facebook.

You have probably heard this saying as well, but the main point I try to make is that what is "written" on the Internet is in INK AND NOT PENCIL. In other words, comments made on Twitter, Facebook and other social media outlets cannot be erased and will "live forever," especially the comments that bring negative attention and headlines across the country. As you know, comments, photos and videos posted on Twitter or Facebook will go "viral" in a matter of seconds and everyone will be talking about what was said or written. Taking down those comments, eliminating Twitter or Facebook accounts won't remedy the problem. The Internet is written in ink – which means those comments and videos will live on in a blog, article or other form in cyberspace and could be found through a simple Google search.

Remember that you are not the average college student. ANYTHING you say that is questionable can become a headline across the country. Once again, no matter how hard you try to correct a social media mistake and "take something back," Twitter comments are written in INK, not pencil, and are rarely forgotten. Ultimately, you will be judged HARSHLY for those comments. Always remember that although some people respect and adore you for your athletic talent and how good you make their school look when you're playing ball, many others do not feel this way. Some people may dislike you because they feel like you attend their college only because you can ball. Others may be jealous of the attention you get because of your skills. And others simply may dislike you just because you are different from them. I realize it's tough enough balancing what's needed to succeed in the classroom as well as on the fields or the basketball court. You don't need the added distractions you cause YOURSELF, especially negative distractions. The key is to THINK before you make comments and hit the "SEND" button. Thinking about the consequences for a few minutes or even a few seconds can save you from years of unnecessary distraction.

CHALLENGE: Today I challenge you to think more about what you post on Instagram, Twitter and Facebook. Even things you post you believe are unimportant can become "viral" at any moment and lead to major distractions for you, your team and your family. What you post cannot be "erased" and can follow you for a very long time. Be careful!

CHAPTER 29

A FRATERNITY CAN BE A GOOD THING

"Every college man ought to belong to some such movement as this. It broadens his horizon and brings him into vital touch and fellowship with college men everywhere." – Elder Watson Diggs, Founder of Kappa Alpha Psi Fraternity, Inc.

In my opinion, African-American male student-athletes should be encouraged to join historically black fraternities (HBFs) or at least take a close look at joining one of them. Yes, I know that there are some big-time horror stories out there about fraternities and what they stand for and the negativity they seem to promote. But from my perspective, African-American fraternities are much more than drinking, hazing, sexual misconduct, drug-use, etc. and parties at the frat house (almost no African-American fraternity chapters own fraternity houses on campuses like many of the historically white fraternities). Fortunately, I grew up in a home where my mother belonged to an African-American sorority as did many of my relatives. So from day one, I got a chance to witness the positive side of fraternity and sorority life.

Coaches, athletic administrators, parents and others should realize the importance of historically black organizations. I do not think it is an overstatement to say such organizations are viewed along with churches, barber shops, and athletics as staples within the African-American community. Like me, many college students are raised in families where becoming a member of an African-American Greek letter organization is very important, particularly if the students' parents, siblings, and/other family members are members of such organizations. Unlike some organizations, historically black fraternities and sororities are life-long commitments that continue years after graduation, many times until death.

Despite the fact that a number of the men I interviewed for my dissertation discussed the positive role their fraternities played in their academic performance while in college, some of them mentioned that coaches often discouraged and even prohibited them from joining fraternities. At least one mentioned that his coach threatened to "pull" athletic scholarships if the players on the team joined fraternities. This is not only wrong, it also cuts them off from important networking opportunities that can help them in the future.

People may be surprised by the number of African-American assistant coaches and athletic staff members who are members of historically black fraternities. More importantly, African-American fraternities can serve as another support system/group for African-American student-athletes. Such organizations can enhance the academic performance of the student-athletes because each organization requires a prospective member achieve certain GPA requirements to be considered for membership. Involvement in community service plays a very significant role within each HBF as well. My own fraternity first introduced me to community outreach programs such as coat drives for children, serving food to the poor during the holiday seasons, food drives and visiting schools to read to children. Athletic departments across the country stress the importance of community service, and the fraternity initiatives are very similar to those within athletics. Besides helping people, a great part of community service is that it makes you realize that life is not all about YOU, and there are always people out there who are less fortunate than you are.

The following influential African-American sports figures are all members of African-American fraternities: Michael Jordan (Omega Psi Phi), the legendary Bill Russell (Kappa Alpha Psi), Pittsburgh Steelers head coach Mike Tomlin (Kappa Alpha Psi), Emmitt Smith (Phi Beta Sigma), Shaquille O'Neal (Omega Psi Phi), University of Texas coach Charlie Strong (Phi Beta Sigma), Philadelphia Eagles wide receiver Jordan Matthews (Kappa Alpha Psi), former Baltimore Ravens linebacker Ray Lewis (Omega Psi Phi) and Myron Rolle (the only Florida State football athlete to ever earn a Rhodes Scholarship – Kappa Alpha Psi). Deceased notables such as Dr. Martin Luther King, Jr. (Alpha Phi Alpha), astronaut Ronald McNair (Omega Psi Phi), attorney Johnnie Cochran (Kappa Alpha Psi), former ESPN sports anchor Stuart Scott (Alpha Phi Alpha), renowned poet Langston Hughes (Omega Psi Phi) and The Honorable Thurgood Marshall (Alpha Phi Alpha), the first black U.S. Supreme Court Justice, were also members of HBFs. Many other lesser-known, but very influential individuals excelling in business, medicine and health care, engineering, intercollegiate and professional athletics, entertainment, and other endeavors can be found within each African-American fraternity.

Black fraternity/sorority involvement has always been a very big part of my life since I was a small child. I have definitely enjoyed being a member of my fraternity for the past 25 years and strongly encourage you to attend at least one fraternity interest meeting on your campus in the near future just to get a feel for what the organization is about. Don't just read about fraternities (because much of what you read may bad) or listen to what your friends say, go find out for yourself.

CHALLENGE: I challenge you to take time to find out much more about historically black fraternities for YOURSELF rather than simply listening to those around you. It's often easy for people to criticize organizations or people they don't know personally or haven't been introduced to, so it is important for you to do your own research when making decisions.

FRATERNITY LIFE

Fraternity Brothers Dr. Derrick Gragg, James Sanders, Patrick Fitch, Clarence Sevillian & Jason Brown – Kappa Alpha Psi Fraternity, Inc.

Dr. Derrick Payne,
Alpha Phi Alpha Fraternity, Inc.

Lt. Colonel William Brown, Jason Brown, Dr. Derrick Gragg, Kappa Alpha Psi Fraternity, Inc.

CHAPTER 30

#16 LIEUTENANT COLONEL WILLIAM E. BROWN, CORNERBACK - "THE LEADER"

"Service to others is the rent you pay for your room here on earth." - Muhammad Ali

Lt. Colonel Brown with Julian Bond and Congressman Tom Perriello

Every group has at least one person who seems to be more focused and serious about achieving great things than the others. From the very beginning, it was evident to me that William was that guy. The first semester at Vandy was a terrible welcome to bigtime college football, at a world-renowned and demanding academic university. During our first semester, most of DaFellaz achieved below average grade-point averages (GPA) except for William, who's GPA was nearly 3.0. Anyone who plays competitive athletics on the highest level knows that earning that type of GPA in your first semester at a university with high academic standards, team practices with increased workout demands, pressure to win, coaches on your back constantly, study hall requirements, and all the distractions of college campus life is quite impressive.

Growing up in the urban areas of St. Louis, Missouri, William escaped many of the dangers associated with his environment by attending a military high school. By the start of his senior high school year, William was a standout athlete in three varsity sports, earned a promotion making him the second highest ranking military officer at the school and achieved academic recognitions including the "St. Louis Post-Dispatch Scholar-Athlete of the Year Award," and was selected by his peers as *Most Likely to Succeed*.

After sustaining a near season-ending back injury his sophomore season at Vandy, William remembered the importance of his post-football career game plan. Battling injuries for the remainder of his college career, made William increase his already-keen focus on the "big picture" and what lay ahead after college. Since he had many other interests outside of football and was conscious of the need to focus on others and to give back to the community, William joined the Vandy chapter of Kappa Alpha Psi, Inc., a national fraternity whose members are prominent leaders in government, civil rights, athletics, business and all other fields of human endeavors. Later as president, he was responsible for ensuring the chapter made a significant contribution to the Vandy campus and the local Nashville community. During his time as president, university officials honored the Vandy chapter of Kappa Alpha Psi, Inc. by naming it "Vanderbilt University Fraternity of the Year" for service to the university and local community. William's commitment to others is inspired by his biological father who fought in Vietnam and returned to a bitter homecoming while wrestling with the post-traumatic effects of war. He struggled but failed in his effort to hold the family together – yet did for others when he could not do for himself.

Like many in our group, a stepfather raised William. William says, "My parents split up, and my stepfather came into my life at a critical time in my development as a young man. He is a strong black man who fought in both the Korean and Vietnam wars. Instilling in me the virtue to be a fighter, he refused to bow down to anybody."

But like many other black men in America, his stepfather has overcome racism and unfair treatment experienced simply because of the color of his skin. William recalls, "After my stepfather returned home to St. Louis after a combat tour of military duty in Vietnam, a white police officer pulled him over for an alleged minor traffic violation (a common tactic then and even today). The policeman pulled him out of the car for allegedly being verbally rude and brutally beat him on the street. Despite being discouraged by acts of police brutality, enduring discrimination on public transportation and facing racism at certain local restaurants and theaters in St. Louis, he still loved America and taught me every day to do the same."

In 1999, William graduated from St. Louis University School of Law and followed the examples of his father and stepfather by answering the call to duty in joining the U.S. Army Judge Advocate (JAG) Corps as a military lawyer. William exceled and rose to become one of the highest-ranking black men in the Army JAG Corps. However, his success comes with major sacrifices. William has served our country as an Army officer for more than 16 years and has been deployed to Iraq and Afghanistan. Awarded two Bronze Star medals for deployments in each combat zone during a time of war, William risked his life to fulfill duties to the Army and to defend our freedom.

As predicted, leading and serving is exactly what William is doing every day. Even today as a senior Army officer, William still takes time to volunteer for community-based projects and is actively involved in many civic, church, and community organizations. He works to persuade troubled teens to avoid gangs, drugs and violence; often serves as a keynote speaker at schools and church youth programs.

There are many ways to serve your country, community and school. As an athlete, you are considered a hero in your hometown. Kids from your neighborhood, friends from high school, neighbors, members of your church and youth from the recreation center you grow up around would all like to have the opportunity you have in front of you. They look to you as a role model. Start BEING that role model by giving back.

CHALLENGE: Today I challenge you to think about your action plan for life after sports and to give back to the community, especially to those in need. Bring hope back to your community and help others achieve the same types of "big things" that you are going to accomplish.

<u>CHAPTER 31</u>

DREAM STEALERS

**"Don't let anyone who gave up on their dreams talk you out of yours." –
Unknown**

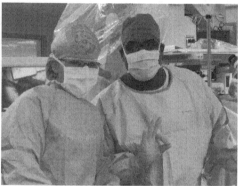

Dr. Frederick Harris - Neurosurgery

Have you ever met people who attempt to define you and tell you just how much in life you are NOT going to accomplish? They tell you who you are, what you are worth (or how little you are worth), and tell you what you are capable of doing. And, most of all, they stand ready to tell you that you aren't nearly as good as you think you are. These types of people are who I call "Dream Stealers." No matter what name you may attach to them (haters, blockers, etc.) they are all very dangerous. Unfortunately, you may encounter these negative people more often than those who have your back, have your best interests in mind and support all those "impossible" dreams you have in your head. You may notice there are

times when the people closest to you are the most negative. The person may be a best friend who didn't do as well as you did in school, a teammate who won't follow team rules and didn't work as hard during the off-season as you did, or a family member who wishes he were in your shoes. Regardless of where the negative vibes come from, you should do everything you can to remain positive and avoid the haters.

Sometimes the road you travel will be filled with more challenges than for others. You will encounter great obstacles along the way, many intended to trip you up and keep you from reaching what I call your "life's destination." One of my best friends from high school, Dr. Fred Harris, who is one of the top brain surgeons in his region, spoke to me recently about the challenges he encountered during his professional climb to the top. Fred and I met while in high school when I began the process of joining a service club/fraternity he had already joined. Although Fred and our other "Big Brothers" were not very kind to us during our pledge process, he quickly became one of my closest friends after the process was over. We remained close during our two years in high school together and continued to stay in touch after he went off to Southern University to study engineering. Fred returned to our hometown to work at the local Army base as an engineer after graduating. After a year or two of working there I helped he and his wife load up a U-Haul truck for their move to Austin, Texas where he went to earn a master's degree in engineering.

A few years after that, I remember visiting him in Columbus, Ohio, where he was a student at The Ohio State University where he was going through a one-year program awaiting admittance into the university's medical school. I remember thinking, "This guy wants to be a BRAIN SURGEON?! How long is this going to take? Is he ever REALLY going to get out of school?" When I think back, I can now see that Fred had a plan and a vision that he was going to reach regardless of the amount of time it took him to get there.

Today, Dr. Fred Harris is a husband who has been married for more than 20 years and is a father of three beautiful, bright children. He also happens to now make more than a million dollars a year as one of the youngest African-American brain surgeons in the country. Despite all the success he has worked for and is enjoying now, Fred told me that during his days as a resident doctor, many of the other surgeons would not talk to or advise him while in the operating room. They obviously did not want him to succeed, they wanted him to FAIL. Fortunately, he noticed very early on that not everyone was on his side. Instead of becoming frustrated and lashing out or giving up, he began listening and observing much more closely when the surgeons would instruct and talk to other residents even though he was given the cold shoulder. Fred had worked too hard to get where he was to just give up. He did what he had to do to learn and better himself despite not having the assistance and help his co-residents received.

Dream stealers will come in all shapes and sizes throughout your lifetime. As you continue to rise toward your goals and dreams, you will probably find that the more successful you become, the more haters will come around to try and bring you back down to their level. Just remember, no matter how "big" you get, how successful you become, or how happy you may end up in life, there will always be someone there waiting to bring you back down to earth. However, you should always continue dreaming of things that are "impossible" and doing things that are unthinkable. You should actually thank God for these people because they may end up motivating you even more. The only person who can really kill your dream is YOU.

CHALLENGE: Today, I challenge you to become even more serious about what you want to do in life and pursue those goals with a passion that most people wouldn't understand. Persist, endure and carry on **NO MATTER WHAT!** Never allow anyone to steal or kill your dreams.

CHAPTER 32

ONE SHINING MOMENT

"Eight seconds, Burton waits, Burton waits, Burton drives... It's good! It's good! It's good! It's good! It's good! It's good! It's good! My God, It's good! My God, It's...So...Good!" – Georgetown basketball radio announcer Dr. Rich Chvotkin's call on WWRC-AM, March 15, 2001

Nathaniel Burton, Former Georgetown Basketball Student-Athlete – Photo Credit: Georgetown Athletics

To me, former Georgetown basketball player Nathaniel Burton is the greatest sports hero of all time ... Wait, WHO?

Out of all the things I have encountered during my career, the most important moment of my life was a monumental event that occurred on a national stage that even the most devoted college basketball fan probably doesn't remember. The date was March 15, 2001 and the particular moment occurred in Taco Bell Arena at Boise State University. As an associate athletic director at the University of Arkansas, I was a member of the travel party for our men's basketball tournament appearance in Boise, where we were playing the Georgetown Hoya basketball team in the first round. We felt very confident about the game, after all, we were a Number 7 seed and they were Number 10, plus, we had Joe Johnson (yes THE Joe Johnson who was drafted 10th overall into the NBA and has played in the league for over 15 years). It was an exciting game and the score was close the entire time. While Nate Burton never became a Georgetown household name in the mold of Patrick Ewing, Allen Iverson, or Alonzo Mourning, during one of his final games as a Hoya, Nate took matters into his own hands for 10 seconds and changed the course of my life forever. With moments left on the game, he drove in and hoisted up a shot at the buzzer. We all thought the shot went up after the buzzer had sounded, but the referees saw it differently. After a lot of protest by the Arkansas faithful and discussion by the officials, the basket counted – game over... Season over. The plane ride home the next morning was a very sad and long four hour stretch. A long plane ride is much worse when you're riding with a group of disgruntled young athletes and an entourage of supporters and alumni who felt that they were cheated out of a victory.

We arrived back in Arkansas and I went straight home to check on my wife who was eight months pregnant. When I spoke to her earlier that day she told me she was going to leave work early because she wasn't feeling well. She went to sleep early that evening, but I stayed up late to write a paper for the doctorate degree I was working on at the time. I finally got in bed around 2 a.m. but was awakened suddenly around 3 a.m. because our bed was literally shaking – my wife was lying across my legs having a massive seizure, her eyes were rolled to the back of her head and she was not breathing. I called 9-1-1 twice but could not get through and finally dialed 1-4-1-1 for the local operator who was able to connect me to the emergency 9-1-1 operator.

"My wife is not breathing!" I yelled into the phone, "Send someone quickly PLEASE!"

"Sir," the dispatcher answered, "the ambulance is on its way, but I'm going to assist you until it arrives. First, you're going to have to get your wife off of the bed and roll her onto her back on the floor."

I dropped the phone and began pulling my wife gently off the bed onto the floor. I began to panic and cry as I lifted her listless body off the bed. After getting her to the floor I picked up the phone again.

"Tilt her head back," the dispatcher said. Miraculously, Sanya began to breathe a bit after I tilted her head back. She was also bleeding from her mouth because she had clamped down on her tongue during the seizure. Her teeth were clenched, so I could not get my fingers into the back of her throat, which is probably what saved at least one of my fingers. Then suddenly, she gasped, coughed and began breathing more normally. As tears ran down my eyes, I thanked the dispatcher who said she would remain on the phone until the paramedics arrived. The five-minute ride to the hospital felt like an eternity and I felt a great deal of relief once we arrived. However, my relief soon disappeared as my wife suddenly began to have much worse episodes of convulsions, causing the emergency room bed she was lying in to shake.

Dr. Cole, one of the most respected "baby doctors" in Arkansas and also a proud Arkansas Razorback alum himself, had done everything he could to ensure that my wife received the best care during her pregnancy. As he entered the room, Dr. Cole extended his hand to me and as he looked at my wife, he said, "Oh my God, she's full blown toxemic! We're going to have to deliver the baby right away." This meant that her blood pressure had suddenly spiked to a level that could kill not only the baby but her as well.

As they began preparing my wife for surgery, I stepped out of the room into a small restroom next door to gather my thoughts and have a talk with the Man Upstairs. Since I was raised in the church, I have always been a spiritual person. I then looked at Dr. Cole and asked, "Doc, do you have a plan?" His nod assured me that he would do everything he could to save them and my wife was whisked down the hallway to the emergency operating room.

The emergency room doctor who had assisted Dr. Cole finally entered the waiting room after what seemed to be an eternity. Without uttering a word, he plopped down in a chair across from me, exhaled loudly and slumped down in the chair. "I didn't think we'd save the baby or your wife" he said. Dr. Cole told me later that morning that had I not been in town to get her breathing again and call for the emergency staff, that my then 7-year-old and 4-year-old would have found my wife dead that morning.

This explains why I am such a huge Nathaniel Burton fan. Because of him, we lost that controversial game the day before. But because of him, my wife and now 14-year-old son are still alive. After the game that night, Nathaniel was quoted as saying, "I was nervous because I thought I got the ball off after the buzzer," Burton said. "But I guess I did." Yes, he did... Thank God he did.

The lesson here is very simple. Always remember, there is NOTHING more important than your family – no championship, no records, no Hall of Fame induction and no multi-million dollar signing bonus. NOTHING is more important than your family. NOTHING!

CHALLENGE: As the saying goes, life is short and can be much shorter for some people. Today I challenge you to reach out to those who mean the most to you. A simple text to say that you're thinking about someone or that you love them can go a long way. Nothing is more important than family and close friends. After all, they are the ones who will be there for you through your ups and downs. Reach out today.

*THANK YOU Nathaniel Burton, wherever you are, and Rest in Peace Dr. Cole.

CHAPTER 33

PAUL ROBESON: THE ULTIMATE STUDENT-ATHLETE

"We don't need more rappers. We don't need more basketball players, No more football players. We need more thinkers." – Tupac Shakur

The legendary Paul Robeson was a multi-sport scholar-athlete who attended Rutgers University. He entered the university in 1915 and became the epitome of athleticism and scholarship. Arguably, Robeson is widely considered an individual who accomplished more athletically and academically than any other student-athlete past or present. He was not just one of the greatest athletes in Rutgers' history, but also one of the best student-athletes of all time. Even before his enrollment at Rutgers, Robeson was valedictorian of his high school class, and a member of the debate and drama clubs and choir at his school.

While attending Rutgers from 1915 to 1918, Robeson was named as an All-American football player twice and earned 12 varsity letters while competing on four different sports teams. (Most of today's college athletes, only compete in one sport with a small number of student-athletes competing in two sports during their college careers). Although he was an amazing all-around athlete, Robeson's academic and extracurricular achievements were even more impressive. In his junior year at the university, he was one of only a few undergraduates admitted to the Phi Beta Kappa Honor Society. As a member of the debate team, he never lost a speaking competition. Robeson was only the third African-American enrolled at Rutgers and was the only Black person on campus during his time there; however, he was class valedictorian when he graduated. Considering the racism, isolation, and economic obstacles he faced, these combined academic and athletic accomplishments are nothing short of astounding. Are there any modern-day "Paul Robesons" out there now? Despite the negative images of student-athletes we often see, I submit that there are definitely modern-day Paul Robesons throughout the country.

Let me tell you about a modern-day Paul Robeson. Throughout my career, I have met many excellent student-athletes. However, I have yet to encounter anyone who maximized the opportunities his football scholarship brought him more than Dr. Rosevelt Noble, or "Rosie," as he is known, and former Florida State star Myron Rolle, who became the only FSU football player in history to earn a Rhodes Scholarship to study at Oxford in England.

I first met Rosie in the early 1990s, when he was a freshman football player at Vanderbilt. At the time, I was a new athletic administrator at my alma mater, working as the primary student-athlete academic advisor. My patience often ran thin with the student-athletes who didn't "handle their business" in the classroom. However, I noticed that Rosie was a bit different than the average "snot-nosed freshman," as we labeled them. I felt an instant connection with him, because even though he came from a very disadvantaged background, Rosie had a PLAN. Rosie walked into my office at Vanderbilt 20 years ago and never left the campus. He earned his bachelor's degree in only three years, a master's degree, and a PhD from our alma mater. Dr. Noble is now a senior lecturer of Sociology at Vanderbilt University where he heads up a major project called "Lost in the Ivy" documenting the college experiences of Vandy's black alumni.

Myron Rolle is another modern-day Paul Robeson. Although I do not know Rolle personally, I have been a big fan of his from afar since I first heard of him a few years ago. Myron was one of the best defensive players in FSU history who was on his way to becoming an NFL player. But his dream of becoming a scholar and a physician were bigger than his dreams of playing in the league. Myron even postponed entering the NFL draft to study at Oxford for a year. He only played in the NFL for three years before retiring to focus on becoming a doctor. He is now enrolled at FSU's medical school where he is studying to become a brain surgeon.

Like Rosie and Myron, I hope you strive to a modern-day Paul Robeson. If not, what can you do to better yourself overall to become more like him? First of all, I challenge you to be the best YOU that you can be. I also challenge you to use Paul Robeson as a role model and take full advantage of all the opportunities you have in and out of the classroom! If people like Robeson, Rosie and others have faced and beaten "impossible" odds, you can, too!

CHALLENGE: Today, I challenge you to do everything you can to take positive steps towards becoming a modern-day Paul Robeson. Study harder, ask for help when you need it and EXCEL in the classroom and in all phases of your life.

CHAPTER 34

DRUGS AND ALCHOL ARE "UNDEFEATED"

"A man will never be strong until he knows what his weakness is. What is YOUR kryptonite?" – T.D. Jakes

I will never forget the documentary that I saw on former college and pro basketball player Chris Herren. Surprisingly, I actually had not heard of Herren until I watched the footage about his life. But after watching it several times, I can say that he is one of the most fascinating, compelling and tragic figures in sports history. This documentary should be MANDATORY education for all college student-athletes. At one time Herren was one of the most highly recruited high school basketball players in the country. He signed with Boston College to stay close to home, his family and his best friends. This seemed to be what fueled his downward spiral into a world of alcohol and drugs.

Herren's drinking and smoking weed led to other more dangerous, high-risk drugs such as heroin, pain killers and crystal meth. Herren was so addicted to drugs that he often used them on game days in the NBA before taking the floor. Fortunately for Herren, he has been able to stop drinking and doing drugs and has been clean the last few years. He now travels around the country spreading his story and educating others on the dangers of drug use. He is very courageous and I applaud him for sharing his experiences. I am sure that he has helped many people with his very candid talks; however, another promising former basketball superstar – University of Maryland's Len Bias – was not so fortunate.

During his playing career, Len Bias was often mentioned in the same breath with other stars such as Michael Jordan and Dominique

Wilkins due to his high-flying acrobatic style of play on the court. Bias was twice named Athletic Coast Conference (ACC) Player of the Year and was also a two-time All-America player for Maryland. After his senior season, Bias was selected second overall in the NBA draft by the Boston Celtics. The day after the draft Bias and his father traveled to Boston to meet with the team owners and management. After returning to campus to celebrate later that night, Bias – and some of his friends and teammates – used cocaine. A few hours later, Bias's heart stropped and he collapsed. After all attempts to save his life were unsuccessful, Bias died that morning from a cocaine overdose. He was only 22 years old. Since I was in high school at the time, I remember this very vividly. I never met Len Bias or anyone close to him, but as a young athlete hoping to play big-time college ball, I could relate to the situation. Today I find myself thinking about that situation from time to time.

Len Bias had MADE IT. He was the "next Michael Jordan" many of us called him. Then, all of a sudden, after a terrible decision to use drugs, he was gone - forever. The list of superstar athletes and entertainers who battled alcoholism and drug use is a long one. Despite their athletic ability, none of them were able to avoid the pitfalls of drugs and alcohol. Think how great they all COULD have been without the drugs.

Today as an athletic director, I notice more athletes testing positive for marijuana, while others have been arrested for possession of drugs. Man suspensions for "violating team policies" can often be traced to failed drug tests. Not many good things happen when alcohol is involved: making a fool of yourself and damaging your reputation beyond repair, rapes and sexual assaults, fighting, and even more violent episodes occur. Also, always remember that no matter how good you are, you will not perform at the top level of your ability if you are under the influence of drugs or alcohol. And, of course, driving under the influence can lead to serious accidents and DEATH. Is having a "little fun" with your friends really worth all of that? I certainly hope not.

Many people who are not superstars or celebrities deal with alcohol and drug addiction every day. None of us are totally immune from it and most of us know people – including family members – who are addicts. Young people (and everyone else who is reading this), please understand that drugs are UNDEFEATED and seek and destroy everyone in their pathway.

CHALLENGE: Today I challenge you to take control of your life as it relates to drugs and alcohol. Don't let a few bad minutes or hours ruin your life forever. If you have a problem that you can't control, please talk to your parents, coaches or anyone you feel has your best interest at heart. You can overcome any problem you have with the right support. If you do not have problems with alcohol or drugs, continue to do the things that have kept you on the right path so far. Ball players can't operate at full tilt under the influence.

*R.I.P. to former Maryland superstar Len Bias. God Bless him, his family and those who cared about him.

CHAPTER 35

#33 ANTHONY CARTER, RUNNING BACK – "THE SURVIVOR"

"Your wins may make you popular, but your greatest defeats will define who you become." – Dr. Derrick Gragg

Photo Credit: Vanderbilt University Athletics

Anthony Carter – or "Ace" as we call him – is the only guy I know who was raised by a single father rather than a single mother. Unfortunately, in the black community, it is not unusual for a woman to raise children without their fathers; but it was unheard of for a single father to raise his child alone, especially during the 1980s. Ace is a former "military brat" who was actually born in Frankfurt, Germany. While in high school in Radcliff, Kentucky, he was a two-sport standout who earned the Conference Running Back of the Year as well as All-State honors in track.

When we got to college, I, myself, had never really lifted weights as a high school player. Ace, though, looked like he could lift a HOUSE. He was powerful and FAST, especially for someone who looked like he was 100 percent pure muscle. Ace reminded me of Adrien Peterson or Bo Jackson in his appearance. He was freakishly athletic and could run a sub 4.4 40 weighing in at nearly 200 pounds as a freshman. I remember the first time Corey saw Ace when we were moving into the freshman dorm. After Ace walked past us, Corey whispered to me, "Man, who is THAT?" and I said, "That's Anthony Carter, a top 100 recruit in the country." Then Corey asked, "What position does he play? And I replied, "Running back." Corey ended the conversation with, "Man, I'm NEVER going to get a chance to play here!"

As I mentioned, Ace was raised by his father, but he was also different from the rest of us because he was a father himself when he came to Vandy. Of course, today it is not that unusual for students who attend college to already have a child, but back in 1988 when I was 18 years old, I had not grown up around or met anyone our age who already had a kid. I could barely tie a neck-tie and Ace was already a DAD. Talk about perspective.

Although Ace was one of the most highly-recruited players in Vanderbilt history, things didn't start off easy for him on the field. He had a bad ankle injury most of our freshman year and then broke his arm during the spring practice during our sophomore year. And even though he earned the Red Sanders Award as the most outstanding rising senior during spring practice, Ace only scored one touchdown his senior year and three touchdowns during the entire four years at Vandy. In the end, Ace only got to carry the ball SEVEN times our entire senior year. For someone who was a top 100 recruit in the entire nation coming into college, Ace's career did not come close to being what we all thought it would be the first time we saw him run the ball.

Despite the adversity Ace has faced, I never heard him complain or feel sorry for himself. I also never saw him frustrated. The biggest life lesson I learned from Ace is that he controlled what HE HIMSELF could control and didn't focus on things he could not control – such as how many times he got to run the football in a game. Ace routinely finished first in conditioning drills after practice and had a work ethic that was second to none. That was all he could control at the time, so that was his focus. To me, if anyone deserved more opportunities to shine on the field than he was given, it was Ace. Like many, many ball players, he didn't get to accomplish what he wanted to on the football field; however, he did something MUCH more important – he became the FIRST person in his family to graduate from college. After graduating, Ace began at Comcast at the ground level in the customer service call center where he worked the second shift. He then went onto installing cable at homes and apartments. Since that time, as we all expected, he has worked his way up the ladder and is now a very highly respected instructor within the company. He is a true family man and role model for his children and THAT is what life is all about.

I always say that life can be very UNFAIR at times. I have heard my mother say, "If nothing bad has happened to you yet, just keep on living!" But it's not the bad things which happen to you that actually define you, it's how you react. The reality is that most of you will not become the superstar athlete you thought you'd become when you got to college. Like you hear all the time, almost none of you will get to play professional ball. However, you can't crumble when you're done playing ball. The key is how you DEAL with your sports career not going so well. What will you do? How will you react when the game is over? I hope you will react like Ace – without fear, without complaining and controlling what you can truly control. I hope you remember him when you are trying overcome the challenges of your life.

CHALLENGE: Today I challenge you to focus on controlling the things you can control: how much effort you give in the classroom, how hard you practice every day and making better decisions. Don't concentrate so much on the things you cannot control. Those will only distract you. Keep your eyes on your goals.

Anthony Carter displaying game jersey from Vandy days

CHAPTER 36

EXCUSES, EXCUSES, EXCUSES...

"Excuses: Losers always have the best ones." – Dr. Derrick Gragg

Have you ever noticed how many guys make excuses when things don't work out right or don't go their way? When a guy drops a pass, the quarterback threw the ball too high, or the ball was too slippery because of the rain. Or when a guy misses an easy basket, it's because his teammate didn't get him the ball in time and he rushed his shot. When he flunks a class, obviously, the professor doesn't like him or any of the other athletes who take her classes. Nothing is ever his fault. Don't you hate that guy? Don't BE that guy!! Own up to your mistakes and shortcomings, "fall on the sword" and apologize if necessary and move on. No one wants to hear excuses – certainly not your coaches or teammates, who also lost the game. Right after games lost or bad practices, the excuses usually come raining down from the guys who didn't do their jobs. "I missed that block because I had to help John with his man and I couldn't get to mine." "I missed that layup because Steve's pass was low and I couldn't concentrate on the shot once I caught the ball."

Listen, no one is perfect. We all make mistakes. Sometimes, we make a LOT of mistakes. But it takes character to own up to one's mistakes and learn from them. When you think about it, the bad things that happen to you are usually caused by the decisions YOU make or the things that you do (or don't do). Your friends or frat brothers didn't cause you to flunk the class, you flunked it because you were out all night with them "living it up" instead of studying. It's not THEIR FAULT, it's YOUR FAULT. So take full responsibility for what you do. You'd be AMAZED at how much more positively people would respond to you. Most people understand younger people "mess up," but they also have little tolerance for excuses. There may be nothing worse than a person who always has an excuse for their failures.

There will be times when you won't do well, no matter how much effort, sweat, or practice you put into something. Are there faculty members on campus who dislike athletes or sports in general? Of course there are. However, you can't allow those people to make you fail. You'll find that people in the "real world" definitely won't have a high tolerance level for excuses. They would much rather hear an apology and a commitment to do better. Always remember this quote: "A winner has a plan, but a loser always has an excuse." You are a CHAMPION who has worked extremely hard to get where you are today. Champions don't make excuses, they make plays. And even when they do mess up, they make up for their mistakes. Don't make excuses, and don't let challenging circumstances turn you into a loser. Keep WINNING!

CHALLENGE: Today I challenge you to leave the excuses behind, get up, get better, and take full responsibility for what you do. NO MORE EXCUSES! Avoid making excuses not and encourage those close to you to stop making them as well.

CHAPTER 37

TRUE PERSPECTIVE – WHAT'S *REALLY* IMPORTANT

"One day you will realize that things mean nothing. All that matters is the well-being of the people in your life." – *www.livelifehappy.com*

**Lorenzo Seaberry, Former Eastern Michigan University
Football Student-Athlete**

As the Director of Athletics of a major college athletic program, I spend a great deal of time meeting and communicating with coaches, student-athletes, donors and many other friends of the institution. None of my days are the same and many are unpredictable. I am usually overloaded with phone calls, text messages and emails while I run from one meeting to the next. However, no matter how busy I am, every now and then something happens that causes me to pause, slow down a bit and put things in proper perspective.

When I was at Eastern Michigan, one of those big moments of clarity came on a typically hectic day. Our head athletic trainer, Steve Nordwall, who oversaw perhaps the most high-risk and important area in college athletics for our department, sports medicine, walked into my office. Steve always kept me up to speed on injuries and other physical or mental challenges our student-athletes may have been experiencing. He also informed me when any student-athlete has come in contact with police or other law enforcement officials. Consequently, I usually braced myself for "bad" news when Steve came to see me.

I could tell by the troubled look on his face that this was not going to be a very good exchange. I began thinking of the endless scenarios that could have happened the day before. Did we lose someone for the season due to injury? Did someone get arrested? Did an athlete skip a mandatory counseling session?

"Derrick, do you remember Lorenzo Seaberry?" he asked me.

"Of course I do. I saw Lorenzo at a football game earlier this season," I responded.

"Well," Steve said with a serious look, "Lorenzo was just diagnosed with a rare form of kidney cancer and the doctors are saying he will live three to seven months, tops."

After a long period of silence, the only response I could utter was "Steve, how old is Lorenzo?"

"He's only 24," he replied.

As athletic administrators we all come in contact with thousands of student-athletes over a period of time, so it is impossible to remember every one. However, Lorenzo MADE you remember him. Those of us who are parents try not to make distinctions between our children by labeling any of them as our "favorites." We do our best to treat them all the same, and love and care for them in the same manner. Since I have many "children" to care for as the athletic director, I have also attempted not make such distinctions. However, Lorenzo has always been a bit different and ranks near the top of my secret "favorite student-athletes of all time" list. Born and raised in Cleveland, Ohio, Lorenzo beat all kinds of odds on and off the field. He was enrolled in graduate school at Eastern and served as a shining example of how a person can maximize their potential athletically and academically through sports.

Lorenzo entered Eastern Michigan in 2005 as an undersized walk-on/non-scholarship linebacker. Anyone who knows anything about college sports can tell you that being a walk-on is the toughest thing a student-athlete can do. They often end up as "practice players" with little-to-no-chance of ever seeing meaningful action in games, and go head-to-head with much bigger, stronger skilled athletes. They work just as hard as the scholarship athletes while paying for their experiences through work-study, loans or employment. Many of them are truly the unsung heroes of their teams.

The 2009 Eastern Michigan football media guide lists Lorenzo as 5'8" 216 pounds, but those of us who knew Lorenzo knew that this was a stretch, at best. However, what Lorenzo lacked in size, he always made up for in heart, work ethic and personality. He did not play during his first year at EMU, but during the next four years he went on to earn a football scholarship and played in 42 games on special teams and as a reserve linebacker, earning four varsity letters. He was also named "Defensive Big Playmaker" for a game in 2007 and earned three additional single-game awards during his career. These are not lofty statistics by any means, but certainly meaningful and significant, especially when considering the long odds he beat to contribute to his team.

We only won eight football games during Lorenzo's playing career at EMU, and did not win a single game his last year on the team, but he always greeted me with his signature big smile. It was the same big smile I saw at the football game earlier this year. As he approached me at the former football players' tailgate tent, Lorenzo was obviously very proud of our team's improvement and wanted to tell me face-to-face.

"Dr. G, I really like what you guys have going on now with the program," he said.

I responded by thanking him for his past contributions to the program. I did not know that our next in-person visit would take place in a hospital, little more than a month later.

I paid Lorenzo a visit on the Monday of Thanksgiving week. We were heading into our last game with a 6-5 record needing to win a seventh to obtain a winning record for the first time since 1995 and secure the first bowl bid for Eastern Michigan since 1987. Many things went through my mind as I drove to the hospital. I tossed and turned all night prior to the visit. Honestly, I didn't know if I had the courage to visit him, but as the leader of the athletics department, I felt an obligation to go. I was also hoping that seeing a friendly, familiar face would help him in some small way. As a father, I dreaded the visit and could only imagine what his parents were going through.

As I entered his room, I found Lorenzo sitting up on the edge of the bed awaiting a nurse who would replace his IV. His mother asked him if I were one of the coaches. He immediately looked up and said, "Naw, he's the AD. Hey, Dr. G, how are you doing?" My first thought was how he would ask me how *I* was doing at a time when he was supposed to be the focus of attention. I didn't want him to talk too much because he needed his rest; but, he began talking once again about how much better our team was and how he'd seen us play on television while at the hospital.

"Dr. G, if I get out of here," he said with his voice trailing off, "I mean WHEN I get out of here, it would be great to be at the bowl game just to be in that atmosphere one more time."

I promised him that I would reserve a spot in the athletic director's suite just for him.

"Ever the fighter," I thought. Before I left the hospital, I gave Lorenzo's mother my business card and asked her if there were anything she needed. She looked me right in my eyes and simply said, "A MIRACLE. And lots of prayer." That statement stopped me in my tracks. I held back the tears as I exited the room. Even before leaving the parking structure at the hospital, I began centering myself, putting all the TRULY important things into perspective. The first thing I did was pray for Lorenzo and his family. Then I got in touch with my daughter in Alabama, just to let her know that I loved her.

Unfortunately, as we have learned throughout our lifetimes, not all stories have great endings. Just three days later, on Thanksgiving morning, Steve Nordwall called to tell me that Lorenzo lost his courageous fight earlier that morning, surrounded by his mother and other family members and friends. Lorenzo Seaberry III died just a month short of his 25th birthday. I am sure that several of his former teammates dedicated the next day's game to Lorenzo. They played valiantly, losing in a heart-breaking 18-12 game to the eventual Mid-American Conference champion Northern Illinois team. However, as big as the loss was for us, it didn't seem so big anymore.

A few days later, I did something that was even more difficult than visiting Lorenzo in the hospital: I attended his memorial "home-going" service in Cleveland. Many of his teammates from high school and college were there, as well as hundreds of other people. The pastor even remarked

that "Only Lorenzo could throw a party like this." I was not surprised that the little guy with the big smile and even bigger handshake and hug could fill an entire church with people who cared about him. The photographs in his memorial program spoke volumes about the life he led, who he was, and what and who he represented. The words listed on the pages with the photographs described Lorenzo as a son, brother, grandson, uncle, athlete, companion, encourager, teammate and friend. He was all of those things and so much more.

CHALLENGE: Today I challenge you to keep things in TRUE perspective. No matter what you feel is important in your life right now, there is nothing more important than your health and your family.

CHAPTER 38

#17 CLARENCE SEVILLIAN, WIDE RECEIVER – "THE CEO"

"Being ready isn't enough. You have to be PREPARED." – Pat Riley

My teammate and fraternity brother Clarence was always prepared and ready, regardless of what he was asked to do. And he worked HARD every day. He wasn't blessed with great speed but he had the best hands of all of us (we still call him "Money Hands" to this day). He took over the starting role at wide receiver when I was being phased out as the starter. We then spent the last two seasons alternating and running the plays in and out of games (this was way before the wristband, hand signal and poster board systems teams use now). When Clarence graduated from Vandy he held several receiving records. He set a single game receiving yard record in his last game as a Commodore with 222 receiving yards and 3 touchdowns against the always highly-ranked Tennessee Volunteers. He also scored on the longest play from scrimmage in Vanderbilt history (88 yards) in that same game and set a record for yards per catch with a WHOPPING 37 yards per touch. Clarence is still in the top 10 of all-time at Vandy in career receiving yards and touchdown catches.

Clarence wasn't drafted by an NFL team but was invited to several mini-camps with the Cincinnati Bengals that summer after graduation. However, when he arrived for the first day of pre-season camp he was released by the team because they were bringing in NFL veteran receiver Mark Duper from the Miami Dolphins. Just like that, his NFL career was over before it started. Ironically, Duper never played for the Bengals because they also cut HIM before the season started only a month after they signed him. Business as usual in the NFL…

Clarence was star receiver even though we were a team that ran the ball 85-90 percent of the time his last three years at Vandy. Although he was a star on the field, he was also an academic superstar, graduating with a degree in MATH. After his short stint in the NFL, Clarence earned a second bachelor's degree in health science from the University of Michigan-Flint. He went on to earn an MBA from Lawrence Technological University and a second master's degree in physical therapy from the University of Michigan-Flint.

Although Clarence was always prepared and ready to go when it was time to play ball, his preparation was most important when he met Phil Incarnati, chief executive officer and president at McLaren Health Care Corporation. Clarence was hired into McLaren Healthcare in Flint, Michigan as a staff physical therapist. After Phil and Clarence got to know one another, Clarence was given the opportunity to enter management. Since then, he has risen quickly through the ranks to become one of the youngest African-American hospital CEOs in the country. Clarence was recently named CEO of his third hospital, McLaren Bay Region, and continues his rise in the medical field. As the saying goes, "Success happens when preparation and opportunity collide." The same mentality and work ethic Clarence displayed is the same mentality he has carried into the workplace since he began at McLaren.

However, you should remember that just because someone has power and has a great job doesn't mean they don't have to GRIND. Clarence's days often begin before 5 a.m. and end after 7 p.m. Both of his daughters have inherited his non-stop work ethic as well, as they have both earned basketball scholarships at Big Ten schools. His oldest daughter signed with Penn State and became the starting point guard for the team. His youngest daughter signed with Big Ten rival the University of Iowa.

Remember that life after sports will be a lot like life with sports; you have to be prepared and ready when called upon to perform. You have to react in practices and games and you will definitely have to react in life to be successful when certain things happen. You must always prepare and continue to get better even to have a SHOT at becoming successful and fulfilling your dreams. Don't get caught "sleeping" and miss out on your shot, because it may be the only one you get in life to make big things happen.

CHALLENGE: Today, I challenge you to grind harder than ever and be totally prepared and ready to go when your number is called! Don't get caught sleeping and miss out on your shot to accomplish big things!

Clarence Sevillian, CEO, McLaren Bay Region Hospital – Photo Credit: _www.mlive.com_

*Photo Credit on first page of chapter: Vanderbilt University Athletics

CHAPTER 39

P.U.S.H.: "PRAY UNTIL SOMETHING HAPPENS" AND LET'S GO TO CHURCH (OR WHEREVER YOU WORSHIP YOUR GOD)

When God leads you to the edge of a cliff, trust him fully and let go. One of two things will happen. Either He will catch you when you fall or He will teach you how to fly! - Unknown

Unfortunately, we now live in a society that tells us we can't talk about spirituality. Why are some people so offended when other people talk about God or being "religious," especially in the world of athletics? Prayer in schools has been banned for many years and the mass prayers before ball games that I remember from my childhood days are a distant memory. I commend the coaches who have their teams pray before and/or after games. Many of the sports our student-athletes compete in can lead to serious injury. The training the athletes go through has also caused the deaths of numerous young people throughout the years. So why be upset if someone chose to pray and have God "present" when they are training, practicing or competing?

There are some things that God must have made: athletes like the great Jerry Rice, Peyton Manning and the timeless Ray Lewis; ultra-talented entertainers like Ray Charles and Stevie Wonder, two of the best musicians in history who rose to the top of the entertainment world without being able to see. Hip hop stars Eminem, Drake and Kanye West are ridiculously talented. Jay-Z has recorded a dozen million-selling CDs and has more #1 albums than Elvis Presley, Michael Jackson and every other music artist or group in history except the Beatles. Amazingly, he doesn't even write down his lyrics. Such genius SURELY couldn't be accidental. Those individuals have clearly worked very hard to get where they are today. But there is something else, there, too – a Higher Being gave those individuals the talent.

Think about how many things had to happen in your own life for you to be sitting where you are today. Think about where you were five years ago. Think about all the other guys you played ball with when you were younger, or when you were in high school. Where are they? Most of them are not where you are right now. Remember that less than percent of the more than a million high school football players is sitting where you are today and even fewer high school basketball players earn athletic scholarships to play in college. So you being where you are right now is a true miracle. Do you REALLY think that it was all accidental or because you were lucky? I don't think so; I think your God has a specific plan for you.

While writing my dissertation to finish my doctorate, I chose to e-mail several former football student-athletes to request feedback about God and spirituality. I asked the questions: Did spirituality/church play a role in your graduation? Most if not all of them answered that spirituality definitely played a major role in helping them keep going through hard times and graduating. Before asking them whether spirituality played a role in their college experiences, I spoke briefly about my own experiences regarding church and spirituality while I was a Division I football student-athlete. I felt that being truthful about my own spiritual state of mind while in college would encourage participants to respond honestly. I mentioned that even though many African-Americans are "raised in the church," many of my teammates and I drifted away from our spiritual roots during our college years. Due to our hectic schedules as athletes, many of us spent any "free time" we had relaxing, watching sports, cramming for exams, partying or various other activities.

Also it was difficult for me and other African-American teammates to attend church services due to the fact that we had mandatory workout sessions on Sundays at 1 p.m. Although many African-American churches near offered at least one service before or after the traditional 10:45/11:00 a.m. services each Sunday, we were less likely to attend those services. For example, many African-American churches held (and still hold) 7:00 a.m. and 8:00 a.m. services. However, it was very difficult to attend the early services during the football season because we played our games on Saturdays. If the games were at night (many games earlier in the season are played at night in the South due to high daytime temperatures) or if we traveled to play on the road at another university, we would usually get to bed very late Saturday night or not until early Sunday morning. Due to fatigue and a 1 p.m. mandatory workout session looming, many of us chose to "sleep in" rather than attend early morning church services. And for anyone who worshiped on Saturdays, attending those services was basically impossible.

Also, from my experience, many African-American church services are longer than most other church services I have attended (some African-American church services routinely last more than two hours). That means if we attended an 11 a.m. service we would either be late for the workout session (which was DEFINITELY not allowed by the coaches) or we would have to leave the service at least 30 to 45 minutes early to drive back to campus, dress for the workout session and be in the weight room or on the field by the designated workout time. Therefore, many of us simply chose not to attend church services. Additionally, players who were injured in any way during the games were required to attend mandatory early Sunday morning sessions with team medical trainers and/or doctors. Thus, it was impossible for injured players to attend church. After a while, a pattern of missing or simply skipping church services became a habit for many of us, even if we played games earlier on Saturdays at our home stadiums.

Since the NCAA mandates that student-athletes be given a "day off" each week in which no mandatory athletically-related activities may occur (e.g., mandatory practice, workout sessions, film sessions, etc.) coaches may want to consider designating Sundays as the days student-athletes rest, attend church services and recuperate. If you are not off on Sundays, you and some of your teammates should talk to you head coach and ask them if he can set later times for practice/workout activities on those days.

My advice to everyone who believes in a Higher Being is to never, ever, let people tell you that your God does not exist. When you finish reading this chapter, I hope you will find a couple of minutes in a quiet place and thank God for all He has done for you, the talent. He has given you and for everyone in your life who has helped you get where you are today. And if you keep believing in Him, praising Him and thanking Him for what He has done for you, you will be amazed at what He will do for you in the future. So don't forget to get up and go to church or wherever you may worship!

CHALLENGE: Today I challenge you to stand strong in your faith and belief in God even though it may not be "popular" among those around you. Give Him thanks and don't be apologetic about it. Stay on the path that your God put you on, because, after all, you would not be here if it were not for Him! Amen.

CHAPTER 40

#1 DR. DERRICK GRAGG, WIDE RECEIVER – "THE TRAILBLAZER"

"I've failed over and over and over again in my life...
That is why I succeed." - Michael Jordan

University of Tulsa President Steadman Upham and Dr. Derrick Gragg at press conference introducing Dr. Gragg as Vice President & Director of Athletics, University of Tulsa - Photo Credit: *Tulsa World*

The word "finish" is one we have all heard many times throughout our lifetimes, particularly those of us who are/were athletes. Many of us have also heard the saying "It's not how you start, but how you finish." That is very true of almost everything in life. Always remember: It often doesn't matter who your mother or father are or where you came from; some of the most accomplished people in the world were born into very challenging circumstances.

Several members of the Da Fellaz have experienced "starting from the bottom." Several of us are from "broken homes" and grew up in one-parent homes. We were definitely not as financially fortunate as our

Vanderbilt classmates. However, failure was never an option for anyone in our crew. To remind myself of where I came from, for the past 15 years or more, I have carried an index card in my day planner that simply has "1.06" written on it. This number has played a very significant part in my life because it represents my grade point average after my first semester as a football student-athlete. Like many people reading this, I quickly learned that there was a MAJOR difference between high school and college, both academically and athletically. Everything in high school seemed to fall into place so easily. I was a member of the National Honor Society, an all-city three-sport athlete, and voted "Most Athletic" and "Mr. Lee High School" during my senior year. However, just a few months later that all changed when I was back-up wide receiver on a 3-8 football team. To make matters worse, I spent the majority of my first semester concentrating almost solely on football and majoring in something I was completely unprepared for in college: mechanical engineering. That semester, I flunked chemistry and calculus and earned a "D" in an introductory-level computer programming course.

That was one of the first true turning points in my life, and I could have gone either way. I was attending a very expensive university and I definitely had to keep my football scholarship to remain a student at the school. The last thing I wanted to do was to return home as a failure after less than a year. More than that, I did not want to disappoint my mother, who always sacrificed to provide opportunities for my brother and me. So I had a decision to make and my decision was to FINISH what I started. Things did not turn around for me overnight, but gradually, over the next three years, I was able to dig myself out of the academic hole I had dug.

After the first semester of my senior year, I was named to the Southeastern Conference All-Academic Team, an accomplishment that is easily one of the most memorable of my life. Today, I am one of the most educated people in my profession in the United States. Like you, I stand on the shoulders of people who have gone before and made my journey a little smoother and less complicated than theirs was. And, I continue to hear that phrase echoing in my head, "It's not how you start, but how you finish."

Trust that I know how tough life can be and how hard it can be to succeed. Some of us were born with far less status than our peers. However, as I mentioned in another chapter in this book, NEVER use your circumstances as an excuse to fail. Do what you have to do to become more focused. Study harder than you ever have. Be more responsible than you ever have. Do whatever you have to do to improve yourself. Stand up, shake it off, and finish what you started! You can do it! I believe in you. Believe in yourself!

CHALLENGE: Today I challenge you to overcome obstacles and challenges that are in your way. Don't focus on how difficult things have been, concentrate on where you are heading and the amazing future that is in store for you. Finish what you started!

Dr. Derrick Gragg and Mother at Dr. Gragg's Huntsville-Madison County Athletic Hall of Fame pre-induction celebration

BONUS CHAPTER – DADDY

My father didn't tell me how to live. He lived and I watched him do it. – Clarence B. Klelland

July 27th… This date probably isn't any different to most people than any other day, but for me, it's a day of reflection and celebration because it is my father's birthday. Sadly, he was only 54 years old when he lost his life after a very long, heroic battle with kidney failure; so unfortunately, he is no longer here to celebrate the day with us. So each year on July 27th, I wake up, thank God for Dad and think to myself how old he would have been had he made it this far. This year was no different, but as I get older, I tend to get a bit more reflective.

According to recent statistics quoted by CNN anchorman Don Lemon, a whopping 72 percent of African-American children are born to unwed mothers. Seventy-two percent… I have to admit I didn't believe this when I first read it. I knew the number was high but I was definitely surprised to find out the number is THAT high. "Whoa" is the first word I uttered after seeing that statistic. Although some fathers are involved in their children's lives, my guess is the overwhelming majority are raised without their biological father playing any meaningful role in their lives. Seven of the 11 DaFellaz in our group were actually raised in households without their biological fathers, including myself. I actually have not spoken to my biological father – who played absolutely no role in my upbringing – for more than a decade. Even more drastically, one of my closest friends and teammates has not seen his biological father since he was 8 years old.

My father (who was actually my stepfather by definition in today's society and not my "bio Dad") was the toughest, most dedicated man I ever knew. Not that he smashed beer cans into his forehead or broke brick slabs with his bare hands. He was tougher and stronger mentally than physically. His long battle with physical illness began at the age of 17 when both of his kidneys failed. Thankfully, he was born into a very large family (12 brothers and sisters) and the brother closest to him in age volunteered to help save my father's life by donating one of his kidneys to him. When I think about it, his brother was just as brave as Dad because this took place during the mid-1960's, long before today's world of modern medicine. Of course, Uncle Billy has always been my favorite uncle because by saving my father's life, he has indirectly saved mine, as well.

I first met my father when I was 8 years old at, of all places and most appropriately, a football field. His son, Phil, was my teammate on a very competitive youth football team. Phil was a year younger, and it was his first year of football. He was a lineman, so he was a pretty big kid for his age. I felt sorry for him because his dad was always the one who yelled the loudest and stayed on his son the most. I can still hear his voice booming as we trudged around the football field running laps. "Come on Phil!!!" he would yell at the top of his lungs. I remember thinking, "Man, give the kid a break, it's hot out here and the poor kid hasn't ever played before." I also remember thinking how glad I was that Phil was the one going home with him and not me.

So, imagine my surprise when I opened our front door one day a few weeks later and the man with the big voice was standing there smiling. As the "man of the house" at the time, I was NOT HAPPY. What was HE doing here, and why in the world did Mama invite him over? But since that day nearly 40 years ago, I cannot remember a time during the remainder of his life that Phillip was not there for me, or even my own children, despite the fact that he was extremely ill the entire time he was with us.

During my sophomore year in high school, Phillip was given only 6 months to live. My mother never told us this and I only found out through a conversation I had with her when I was an adult. This man underwent kidney dialysis treatment three days a week for 16 years, but never missed one of my college home football games. And the only time he missed my high school games was when he was attending Phil's games since Phil played for a rival high school in the city. This man was EXTRAORDINARY in every sense of the word. A simple handyman who could fix any appliance on the planet. Even when he was sick, he'd go home after his treatments, take a nap, get up and go to work. And he did this repeatedly, day after day, week after week, month after month, year after year. After a lifelong hard fight, we finally laid him to rest in 2001. But I still think about his influence on my life, and how he changed it forever. And although my biological father never attended any of my games, my high school graduation, college graduation or any of the many important events throughout my life, I always had Phillip as a strong father figure and steady male presence in my life since the day I'd met him.

What I realized later in life is that Phillip yelled at Phil so much when he played because he wanted to see him do the things on the field he never got to do. He wanted to see him become a star athlete and earn the football scholarship that he never got the chance to earn himself. He also wanted him to get the college education that he never got himself. And Phil did not disappoint him. He earned a football scholarship to play college ball at Tuskegee University, a very prestigious historically black university, the year after I went to Vandy to play ball. He also fulfilled Dad's dream of earning a college degree.

Trust me, I know how hard it is to become a man without a man around to guide you. What I want to stress is that you shouldn't let growing up without a father, or fathering a child yourself early in life, be an excuse for you to fail to do everything in your power to succeed. And you definitely should never fail your own children in the future. If your dad isn't around, look to other men in your family, your community or your school that you respect, including any coaches you look up to. It can even be a neighbor or one of your boy's fathers. Connect with men who build you up, motivate you to do your best and provide positive support. Remember that despite the dismal statistics quoted at the beginning of this chapter, there are many men out there who overcame great obstacles and became extremely successful, my teammates included. For those of you who have great relationships with your own fathers, please don't take that for granted. There is nothing better than a young man having a positive connection with his father.

CHALLENGE: Today I challenge those of you who have fathers who are not a part of your life to find another mentor/father figure role model whom you respect to help guide and support you. If your father does play a role in your life, respect him and hold onto him. He will be the most important man throughout your lifetime. Remember that even the strongest, most successful men need other men they can look up to and learn from.

*Rest in Peace Uncle Billy and thanks for having the courage to help save my dad. I know the two of you are reminiscing in Heaven as we speak!

Dr. Derrick Gragg and Father James "Phillip" Turner, 1991

Dr. Carlos Thomas

Clarence Sevillian

**Oscar
Malone III**

**Jason Brown
(left)**

Marcus Wilson

Lt. Col. William Brown

Dr. Derrick Payne

Dr. Derrick Gragg

Corey Harris

Anthony Carter

PHOTO CREDITS: VANDERBILT UNIVERSITY ATHLETICS

Dr. Derrick & Sanya Gragg

ABOUT THE AUTHOR

Dr. Derrick Gragg was named Vice President and Director of Athletics at The University of Tulsa (TU) in March 2013. Prior to his position at TU, he was Athletic Director at Eastern Michigan University (EMU) for seven years. Gragg's experience spans 22 years in progressively advanced roles at the University of Arkansas, University of Michigan, University of Missouri and Vanderbilt University.

A former collegiate wide receiver, Gragg lettered four years at Vanderbilt University while earning his degree. He graduated with a Bachelor's in Human Development in 1992 and was a member of the Southeastern Conference Academic Honor Roll during his senior year.
He earned his Doctorate in Higher Education from the University of Arkansas (UA) in May 2004.

Gragg has published several articles and editorials on intercollegiate athletics, as well as a nationwide study on sports-related gambling. He is also the author of the doctoral dissertation, *Factors that Positively Affect Academic Performance of African-American Football Student-Athletes Who Graduate from Southeastern Conference Institutions*.

A native of Huntsville, Alabama, Gragg was inducted into the Huntsville-Madison County Athletic Hall of Fame in 2010. Gragg's wife, Sanya (formerly Whittaker), also earned a Master's degree in Sports Administration at Georgia State University, and a Master's degree in Social Work at the University of Southern California. The couple has four children: daughters, De'Sha, and Saniyah; and sons Avery and Phillip-Raymond.